THE DEER IN THE WOODS AND THE FISH IN THE POND

LIFE SHOULD BE SIMPLE

TOTINO RAMEN

outskirts press

The Deer in the Woods and the Fish in the Pond
Life Should be Simple
All Rights Reserved.
Copyright © 2020 Totino Ramen
v1.0

The opinions expressed in this manuscript are solely the opinions of the author and do not represent the opinions or thoughts of the publisher. The author has represented and warranted full ownership and/or legal right to publish all the materials in this book.

This book may not be reproduced, transmitted, or stored in whole or in part by any means, including graphic, electronic, or mechanical without the express written consent of the publisher except in the case of brief quotations embodied in critical articles and reviews.

Outskirts Press, Inc.
http://www.outskirtspress.com

ISBN: 978-1-9772-0805-7

Cover & Interior Images © 2020 Olivia Voelkel. All rights reserved - used with permission.

Outskirts Press and the "OP" logo are trademarks belonging to Outskirts Press, Inc.

PRINTED IN THE UNITED STATES OF AMERICA

Dedication

In loving memory of Lily Korinne Voelkel, Travis T. Voelkel, Jr., Travis Voelkel Sr., Evelyn Beaumier Voelkel, Carol Lynn Voelkel, all my family on the said side and all my friends like Neil Franke, Brandon Maynard and all soldiers, marines, special ops, airmen, merchant marines and coasties. Also, in memory of all first responders and public servants lost in the line of duty. You will be remembered and we are eternally grateful. No words can express, "Greater love hath no man than this… that a man/woman lay down their life for their friends." John 15:13.

"Every day is an opportunity to grown, love, learn and develop relationships… happy and productive relationships with God, family and friends."

Table of Contents

The Adventures of Totino Ramen: Book One: The 99% Rule: "Being Poor and Not Knowing It."	1
Liam's Ninja Worm	12
The Deer in the Woods and The Fish in the Pond	17
That's Big Game for a Little Kid…Kid with a Pellet Rifle	24
Excuse Me, Thank You, No Thank You, Yes Ma'am, Yes Sir, You're Welcome, I'm Sorry, I Apologize, Yes Please, and Forgive Me	47
"I Did That for Lunch Money": A Rambling Yet Ordered Mess	51
Loonie Farm Adventures	60
31 Days to a Womans Heart	69
I Prefer to Pee Outside	76
Yummy Yummy Says My Tummy	80
Guns Don't Pull the Trigger	95
Mighty Mystical Magical Majestic Musical Mountain Maple Tree	101
Of The Hunt and of The Harvest	105

The Adventures of Totino Ramen: Book One: The 99% Rule: "Being Poor and Not Knowing It."

There was once a family, who most in the community thought were filthy rich, were none other than people who had a lot of assets but little liquid revenue. The family will have the last name Ramen, and the first name Totino...as you know, they were very poor. The kids' clothes came from Good Will or the local thrift stores and occasional new shoes for the year at Payless shoe source. Life was good however, they always had something to eat, if it were something or nothing too fancy, and they had clothes on their backs and were able to go skating at the rink or to the movies for matinee on the weekends....and other not too expensive or too outlandish things done for recreation during their free time. Free time was usually at 9:30 Sundays....after going to the early sermon then heading home to get a fishing pole and catch some bait and go panfish and bass fishing with a bobber and small hook so they could catch the small fish as well as the largemouth bass weighing up to 2.5 pounds. They always had a home cooked breakfast, lunch and dinner on Sundays. My mom would make the most amazing sticky pecan rolls you have ever had and the best homemade banana nut bread that went oh so well with a glass of whole milk. Totino Ramen was the nickname for this family about to be described in this short story. You see, Totino's pizza is the cheapest pizza to be bought at the grocery store, even at Wal Mart or Costco. Ramen is the infamous soup that all poor college kids survive on for their time in college. You see, this family, Totino Ramen did not even know how poor they were until when the kids were old enough to spend the night over at one of their friends' homes and then they are exposed to how other people live their lives and what choices they made to get there and how stressful it is to be in their shoes. The kids would see their friends living in castles, friends living in shacks and places where it was so spooky you could have a heart attack.....They would eat ribeye's and filets and on the other end...home-made spaghetti with garlic bread which was no other than fake butter spread on the toasted bread then dusted with garlic salt or powder. You will see air Jordan's and other expensive shoes and you will see Champion and Winner's choice or Pro Wings. You will see large tv's and not many books....as opposed to the poor home, you will see lots of books and educational resources and less electronic devices and entertainment. This could be the logic behind remaining complacent in life in general or wanting more and to reach for the stars.... with the old adage that education can unlock doors for opportunity.... after completing 4 degrees of which three came from a major university, Texas A&M. Education, of course is earned…..a real education is where you love what you do for a profession and know your area of focus like a master…..a decent education is where you are timid in your application of your skillset and a poor institution is one in which you don't know anything, can't even b.s. your way through a subject conversation and can impress an interview committee but can't even boil rice. NO education can be any one of these traits and education is not needed to be successful…. it is the norm to think that, but it does not matter that much. Look at just two people who dropped out of college…. Harvard at that…. both Bill Gates and that other guy who owns Facebook……yes, both dropped out of college……and they are two of the wealthiest men on earth…financially….at least. Education really starts at home…. how your parents delegate chores around the house…how the kids study every night of the school week…how the kids get a part time job to see what it means to put food on the table and to struggle as a family. My family was just like the Totino Ramen family. We were the 99% rule of being poor and not knowing it. We were trained on shopping for food and clothes, like knowing what to buy at the grocery store since having a job there….like for lunch…a banana and an apple and a piece of French bread………like knowing which off brand lunch meat is the best deal…that would be Carl Budding. Like stealing the neighbors Sunday paper for all the coupons and specials and using all the coupons for grocery shopping. We never had a completely full fridge, but we always had something to eat. For example, during the summer vacation from school, my mom would get us like 25 ramen noodle soup packets for lunch while she was gone to work. We also ate peanut butter and jelly sandwiches which my big brother age 10 would make for my younger brother and me. I was 7 and my youngest brother is 4 and my older brother would cut off all the crusts and make finger sandwiches for us and we would sit on the barstools in the kitchen and eat as brothers. Then we would watch television shows like Gilligan's Island, I Dream of Genie and Mr. Rodger's Neighborhood. All these shows would teach us values and how to think outside of the box. I attribute what we watched to us having over 15 Bachelors and Advanced

Degrees from a two major SEC Universities.

My Family is Totino Ramen to the "T". I am Totino… and referring to family will be named from now on the Ramen's. This will be the first book of many written under that pen name also…Totino Ramen.

Totino was a freshman in college at a major SEC (South East Conference) University and back then, Carl Budding processed lunch meats would cost 50 cents a pack and would have enough meat for 2 -3 sandwiches…if you only had white bread and American cheese on a good day…on an average day be thankful for a few slices of white bread and a squirt of mustard…and a loaf of bread would be store brand and barely under a dollar a loaf, especially from Wal-Mart or H.E.B.…..now dollar stores, 99 Cents stores, and Aldi's have good cheap bread and now even wheat bread is the same price as white bread. Back then, wheat was like what organic is today…more expensive and supposedly healthier…in reality Organic is anything that has a carbon base…so that is everything on Earth that is carbon based and I know for sure is the epitome of organic…not these gimmick Non-GMO and free range articles for purchase at a much higher premium price.

I remember having a large coffee pot.…I would make fresh coffee, teas, soups, like ramen and vegetable and chicken noodle and tomato soups and also grits and rice and oatmeal and boiled eggs which took a while. Those were the days of having it all and yet at the same time, not having it all. The 99% rule in full effect…it really is in the eye of the beholder. Life really is simplicity to a "t" and having time to drink the tea…and having time to do what you enjoy is the benefit of simplicity…too much responsibility and you are stressed, overworked and tired of the everyday grind…just looking forward to weekends, holidays and vacation days off from work. Simplicity does not include board meetings, million-dollar deals…. dealing with powerful people….it means having a fun and rewarding job with excitement and joy….and of utmost pleasure and happiness and not mundane or boring. Just think that there are 99 people better off than you and 99 people worse off than you…that's the 99% rule of logic…..so when you think you have it rough…just think of the 99 you are better off than and pray for the 99 that are worse off than you. If you have $15.00 in your checking account, in your purse or wallet then you are richer than 85% of the world's population. That's three-quarter pounder with cheese burgers and fries and small drink at McDonalds….you see….you don't need to be a millionaire to be rich…just having 15$ in your possession makes you VERY rich. For Totino Ramen and his family, they might have had everything they needed but they were by no means rich or wealthy.

One time, as a child, the middle son and youngest son of The Ramen family both ate raw, uncooked and very bitter acorns for a snack outside their supposedly very wealthy grandparent's home and both got sick to their stomachs from the bitterness of the tannic acid of the acorns. You see, they were thinking like Native Americans….you see…. Native Americans would boil, mash, dry and make flour out of the acorns and bake the bread or fry it and make a great carbohydrate for their meals. You see…. when you are hungry, you get ingenious and very creative…. just like when you are in a real job like the military or civilian sector…but more so in the Military. You get very creative and think more outside the box just like the two kids eating acorns…. you see…you get creative and fill in the gaps of the boiling/purging and grinding of the acorns to make flour with experience….without experience you will want instant gratification and will eat the raw acorns…. you see…with experience comes by thoroughness and diligence in problem solving and this is what life is all about. Life is not all about getting rich or getting famous…it is about survival for the majority of the Worlds population.

Most people to include 1 in 5 Americans does not have a meal each day…no…not even one meal. That is why the profits from this short story will go to feeding the poor, first, in my community, then county, then state, then nation then worldwide. I want to ensure that everyone has access to fresh drinking water and fresh fruits and vegetables and high-quality protein like fish and chicken and beef and goat to eat a few times a week. You see, there are a lot of families like the Totino Ramen's and they need to be taken care of. Most of us take for granted having a job, a home, a vehicle and clean water and a full fridge and freezers full of food.... little to our recognition that over 20% of U.S. Citizens go hungry every day. This is absurd in today's day and age and should be rectified and solved once and for all. I think that every purchase made at a fast food place or restaurant should pay a tax on convenience that goes straight towards food banks and distributors to curb the high incidence of hunger not only in the U.S. but across the globe. Going to school, from grade school to high school and even college as a Freshman thru Senior meant being hungry. You see, Totino's parents were struggling to make ends meet.....he would, most of the time, go hungry or bring a humble lunch of one slice of bologna with mustard on white bread.... yet Totino was very blessed and appreciative and never complained to his parents and was very thankful. He would watch his peers and friends eat their cafeteria lunches...not being jealous or envious. Totino made friends very easily since he was a likeable person. When Totino was in school, he looked forward to playing, not studying, and he was so smart and gifted that he was put into Gifted and Talented classes. He did this for a year or two and confided in his mother that he did not like the way the "Smart" kids would treat other kids at school, like they were superior or better than the other kids that were not as smart...so he opted to go back to regular classes. He excelled at his curriculum and ended up, at high school graduation, top 10% of his class. He did take honors and advanced classes in high school.

Back to Totino Ramen. For breakfast every day of his schooling he and his brothers would drink a glass of whole milk or a humbled bowl of off brand cereals. One time, Totino convinced his loving mother to buy a box of Cap'N Crunch cereal since there was a chance for winning an Atari Game System. Little Totino had two boxes to choose from and guess what, he chose a box with a winning ticket for a free game console. It took two weeks after mailing in the coupon for the Atari to arrive in the mail. Totino and his brothers would master every game that they played, and this kept the boys occupied on days/weekends when it was bad weather outside, preventing them to play.

Back to school and Totino's adventures. He and his brothers would go school shopping, and they loved it....we all knew that our parents were poor so we were thankful when we could get new shoes for the entire year and folders and pens and pencils and paper and we loved every minute of back to school supply shopping. Totino and his brothers enjoyed school. We rode the bus.

When Totino was 5 years old, he wanted to ride the bus with his older brother. Little Totino told his mom how he was a big boy and was old enough to go to school by himself. So that Monday in August, he got up at 6:30 and got dressed and ate his breakfast and waited outside for the bus...number 883. The Bus Driver picked up Little Totino and his brother and they were off to school. When Totino was dropped off, he was disoriented and could not find his classroom for Kindergarten. He waited outside on a bench. Little did Totino know that his mom had followed the bus all the way to his school. As he was crying, his mom walked up and said, "Let's go to your class". That's the kind of mom Totino Ramen had. He never had to ask to find his class again. Little Totino was a great student and very friendly although he usually spent time with only a few select friends, but they were not just friends, they were best friends. He had one friend that was black, one Hispanic, one white, three Oriental kids and some other kids that were mixed. He did not discriminate and was never and is never racist, except when telling crude jokes for comedy purposes. Totino was a good kid and did his chores during the week so that on the weekends he could go fishing with neighbor kids, well about 2 miles away and they would fish and catch fish for the Ramen family...and other poor families indirectly when Totino would fillet loads of fresh fish and the Ramen's froze some and they gave the rest to a poor black family down the road. The black family was so poor that they got our hand-me-downs...that says a lot since we usually wore our Thrift Store clothes and Payless Shoes for over a year or until we were a larger size due to growth. The one who got the most hand-me-downs was Totino's little brother. The other kids at school were dressed in jeans and a t-shirt while the Ramen's wore khakis and nice dress shirts and a nice leather belt. EVERYONE thought the Ramen family was very wealthy since their grandparents were well off and they always wore the nicest of clothes to school and to church. You see...this is the 99% rule in effect. He would eat at the cafeteria for school lunches in the 3rd grade all the way thru 12th grade. Totino was so poor in high school that on most days he would only eat a cherry sweet roll or a pack of zingers for a cost of 50 cents apiece.... on special occasions he would get a chili cheese Frito pie with jalapenos and an iced sweet tea for lunch. He was happy and did not even think that he or his family were poor. He always wanted a truck so that he could haul things, go off-road and do serious hunting and fishing and stow away all of his gear. He would use about a quart of motor oil per week to keep the oil full according to his dip stick. He hauled more with that old 77 Chevrolet C-10 with a bored out 350 V-8 motor. Totino kept this truck for about a year then bought a used jeep Cherokee 4x4 with a small 4-cylinder motor. He re-did all the motor and four-wheel drive and re-did the paint and interior and new cd player and carpet, headliner, seats and new tires and rims. It was a clean and nice jeep for a high school kid. It took 6 months of working on this jeep until it was ready. One day when there were no other vehicles to drive and Totino was still working on his awesome but very used jeep, Totino drove into town while he was re-doing the seats and sat on a 5-gallon bucket. I think that the importance for going to town was for a roll of Copenhagen Snuff. Maybe he also went to Sonic Drive In for an extra-large Cherry Coke...now it is a Route 44 Cherry Coke but now I go with light on the ice...meaning that they did not have this option back in those days...is there evolutionary language creation caused by the Fast Food Fever??? Yes, "The Fast Food Fever". Is going to be a name of a future comedy short story. He ended up selling the same remodeled jeep to the guy he bought it from for a 6 thousand-dollar profit....and his mom split the cost for a newer jeep wrangler with a hard top and excellent four-wheel drive components. Well, that's not how she remembers it.... she remembers that I gave her the money from selling the jeep that I built and gave her the money to support feeding our family. I forgot about that little detail. My Mom actually surprised me at College, behind the dorms, near the washeteria and in the parking lot with a sign saying..... Parking Without a Permit Could Cost You! My little Brother was there too...and my big brother who was a Senior at this University and I was a Freshman. They all said lets go out to eat and spend time together. My little brother was 15 and he was taller than me and I was 18...and we ran to the end of the dorm area and b.s.'ed for a few minutes until everyone else had caught up. We walked the rest of the way and when we got to the parking lot... there was a Jeep Wrangler, my dream vehicle at the time, the elite four-wheel drive, the ability to go anywhere and luxury for an off-road vehicle in those times. It had a maroon bow tied to the rear spare tire. I looked at the jeep, I did not see my mom's Jeep Cherokee or my brothers mustang....so I started yelling at full capacity and then they took a picture of me in that jeep and I was so excited. It needed some better tires, for me, off-road tires, and the ones on that jeep were snow tires, not mud tires and they were halfway thru their tread life. I did end up driving it for a whole year until I needed new tires....and I paid over $800.00 for them at Discount and 18 years later, for a Ford F150 FX4 Platinum, BF G ALL-TERRAIN TIRES...THE BEST tires good for $900.00. This just goes to show you that things are costing more. We then all crammed into the jeep and drove across campus to villager or rather parent visitors weekend and we loaded half of the crew in my mom's jeep Cherokee and half the crew in my new 4.2 Liter 258 In-line six-cylinder 4x4 jeep Wrangler with a stick shift. We enjoyed an expensive dinner of steak, potatoes, salad and green beans and my mom paid for it all. I am not sure how long she went without taking a lunch break and how many hours of work at her second job. Yet, she did pay for it with her love. The same for the meal as was for this expensive jeep. I later found out that while my mom was working two jobs and taking care of a family of 5 and to include multiple pets. She had been investing in real-estate and even had her broker's license. She had 5 townhomes in a worse part of Houston off of highway 59 south. It was her way of showing the world...."You bet the odds were stacked against me.... but I am a proud woman of color and anything is possible with love, and with God." Little did my mom know...she was supporting for the next twelve years in a row...at least two kids in college at an elite University in Texas. We were not considered poor now that we were graduating from college every couple of years...we were considered middle to upper-middle class. We were still acting like we were poor yet becoming more capitalistic as we were aging and more and more educated. Now all of our family can bless one another and many other people we know and haven't quite yet met...with many blessings and happiness and joy. If I were to become a millionaire or billionaire then I would make sure my church gets 10%, my place of worship gets enough money to re-build and my family and friends would each receive a lump sum of cash to ease their financial burdens. I would also save a certain amount of money so that I could live a good and comfortable life of peace and quiet and a time where I could pursue my educational dreams and go to PA or Veterinary school and become a Physician's Assistant in Psychiatry or a DVM in large animal surgery and animal behavior specialist. The dream of having this become real is just a few decisions away. I am taking off this year to get my health back and relax and just do menial tasks here on the farm and at the rental properties. I am content, just going fishing a few days out of the month, especially since it is too hot and there is too much vegetation on all of our fishing holes. Fishing will have to resume when the temperatures get cooler and bearable for spending that much time outdoors. So, we muster up enough energy to do a few important things during the day and then work inside most of the day...only having enough energy to water a portion of the total needed irrigation for our plants, flowers and trees. This is life in a nutshell...hot and cold...brazen and bold... young and old...get weak catch cold. I would ascertain that I admit I still eat Totino pizza and Ramen Noodle soup although it is not on a regular basis. I make it in a microwave now…back then all I had was a coffeemate coffee maker and it would take a while to cook ramen with such little heat…it was awesome…I could make boiled eggs, spaghetti and sauce, oatmeal and beans and rice…I could cook practically anything…it would just take a helluva long time to do it right. I even made macaroni and cheese. I guess I really was poor a long time ago and the little money I do make now seems like a lot since I made very little back then. Life is like that…when you are young you have all these dreams…then you get older and your priorities change…you become more family oriented and more emotional…unless you are successful and are still trying to climb to the top of the ladder, then you will not change much if at all. I made $4.25 and hour…I would work two jobs, one during the week, M-F 3-9 p.m. then one the weekends, 7-7 and on call if emergency fueling was necessary. I made a whopping 75$ on every weekend and I would give this paycheck to my mom to run the house. Yes, we were poor. Totino Ramen poor. Now we are upper middle class and are realizing that money is not as important once you have enough of it and are living a comfortable lifestyle. Back then we would have BBQ-sauce and bread as an appetizer, now we dip hot wings in ranch or bleu cheese…see how times have changed all because of hard work, sticking together and taking care of one another. This is the real adventure…Making Memories out of special events in our lives and also by making a difference in our Communities, State, Nation and World-wide. GOD BLESS THE WORLD…BUT MORESO… THE GREATEST NATION ON EARTH…THE united….UNITED… STATES OF AMERICA….RLTW…..AIRBORNE ALL THE WAY!!!!!!!!!9

Liam's Ninja Worm

One summer day, Uncle Beau and his little brothers kids, yes, all four of them went fishing at a private pond and had live earth-worms for bait. At first nothing was biting but as the scent of the worms in the water, on a hook got dissipated in the water, the action of Bluegill hysteria began. Liam caught the first fish, then Sophia caught one then Olivia then Gavin caught one, yes, his first fish was a beautiful bluegill with the most vibrant colors. This first fish as all of my nieces first fish is getting mounted and will be hung on his wall in his bedroom to remind him and all the other kids in the family of how much fun and love that Uncle Beau has for his brothers kids. Sophia caught four fish that day, most of the group. Liam let her use his rod and reel since we ran out of live worms and had already caught 10 perch for frying up for dinner. He had that worm thru two perch caught and he handed the pole to Sophia since she really wanted to catch another perch…she caught 3 on the same worm. Generally, the worm is eaten by the only fish that it hooks, and you have to re-bait the hook with another worm. Liam had caught 2 perch and Sophia kept the NINJA WORM on the hook to catch 3 more perch…I think this is a fishing record, 5 perch caught and landed with the same worm…hence the term NINJA WORM.

This worm is a runt worm in the box and was saved until last since we thought it was too small to really be bait. You see, sometimes being the oddity or rarity that you are can be a blessing in disguise. Everyone is created equally and differently at the same time. We share the love of one another when we are young and innocent, but then corrupted by criminality in society and we lose that innocence and pick up bad traits or habits that we learned from the criminals in society. When we were ready to go, Liam caught another good-sized perch for our stringer. The funny thing is that Liam's Ninja Worm was still on the hook when it was time to go….as we did, we honored Ninja Worm by letting him live without the box and fridge and be set free by the ponds edge, in the cool, black and thick mud where he or she would live out the days of their lives happy and free.

This "Ninja Worm" lived to see another day. Sure enough, three days later Uncle Beau and Mr. L.C. Crawford went fishing there again and what did they use for bait…. yes…. earth worms from the Styrofoam Box from the bait shop. They fished for hours with 12 worms from that entire box and finally had a full stringer of panfish to eat for supper, enough for 4 people. They both wanted to fish some more so Mr. L.C. got a shovel out of the bed of the truck and he started digging….and he dug near the area where Uncle Beau put the Ninja Worm a few days

prior. Mr. Crawford yelled really loud and said, I got a worm. He brought it to me in excitement and I knew right away that this was the Ninja Worm. Out of respect, Uncle Beau let the Ninja Worm go and they just used artificial jigs to catch two more perch before going home after a good, relaxing and successful fishing excursion. When we put the Ninja Worm by his hole at the banks edge, he let out a Sayonara and gladly went back into his home. He came back out and showed us his black belt and he advised us that anytime we had trouble with any of our worms or any bait that spoke worm then he would handle the situation with as much or as little force necessary. He said he would be our master baiter from now on. He just told us on one condition.... that we never use him as bait when we run out of bait...no matter how desperate we were. He bowed to me and I, likewise, bowed to him and that was our binding contract...the old-fashioned way...but not with a handshake this time, since Ninja Worm does not have hands, we just bowed. After coming to this agreement, we all loaded up the truck and drove home to clean the fish. After arriving home, we took pictures of our catch then went into the house to get two spoons and two filet knives. We used the spoons to de-scale the perch then gut them with the filet knives and slice the sides of the fish to have slits for the seasonings to stick. We washed the fish several times in cold water then marinated them in lime or lemon juice with seasonings, such as chili peppers, garlic, ginger and pepper. We would start a skillet with a quarter to half an inch of melted butter or Crisco in the iron skillet and get the heat up to where the oils are popping when you throw some spices in the oil....in order to test it. Then you would take two perch that are cleaned and seasoned and fry them whole, with the head and all and fry them until golden brown and crispy yet flaky meat just falling off in tender, delectable and good food for ya' white meat. In another pan with butter a sizzlin', we would fry potato slices and season then with only salt and pepper. In a pot, we are steaming some collard or mustard greens and getting ready for plating up the fish and greens and potatoes. This meal is courtesy of L.C. Fisherman's Group LLC, Central Texas. We have this kind of meal about 3 times a month. One day of the month we do something different from fishing...

like rabbit or squirrel hunting. Whenever I need a pick me up or just a quick reset from all the daily and weekly stressors of working, fishing for bluegill and other panfish and keeping some for supper is the greatest benefit of living in the country and having the opportunity to hunt and fish. There was a scientific study that states that kids who fish on a regular basis or hunt on a regular basis, do better in the sciences and math and also sports activities. Their attentiveness and attention to detail is in the top percentage and they are more responsible than kids that do not have weapons like pistols and expensive fishing gear that is to be taken care of properly. There are many things about being an outdoorsman/woman. One being that we could literally survive without any grocery stores. We would be canning all, kinds of vegetables during the growing and harvesting seasons. We would not need to worry about guns and having enough ammunition…since we are well stocked and could stay that way for about 50 years of hunting for food on a regular basis. We have all the camping gear needed to survive a catastrophic situation. This is all due to being one with nature and enjoying hunting and fishing on a regular basis. Long live the Ninja Worm!!!!!!!!!

The Deer in the Woods and The Fish in the Pond

WRITTEN BY: TOTINO RAMEN
FEBRUARY 9TH, 2019

THE DEER IN THE WOODS

There once lived a family of deer in the middle of the woods. They foraged for browse, mast and other good things to eat and to live healthy lives. There was a father, a mother, three aunts and one uncle. The fathers name was Big Rack Buck and the Uncle was Little Spike Buck. The oldest aunt was named Dough, the middle aunt named Doe and the youngest aunt named No-doe. They were all sisters and related to Big Rack Buck and Little Spike Buck.

The two bucks would get along great until their hormones were sky high during something called the "Rut". During this time in winter, they would fight each other and compete for breeding rights for the doe in their family and in other herds in the area. The deer family was beautiful but like all other families, had their up's and down's. Little Uncle Spike had issues with having such a small rack. He felt insecure and never got to breed that many doe in the herd…. unless Big Rack Buck was not around, or any other larger buck was not around. This was how the deer would pass on their genes so that their DNA (Deoxy-Ribo-Nucleic-Acid) could be passed on to their potential offspring.

It was a good breeding season for Big Rack Buck. He was a typical male buck with a nice rack that the doe he proposed to, breed, and chase during the rut and fell in love with him. Looks are typically the main reason why doe breed the good looking and dominant bucks, even though they might have bad traits of anger, hostility, rage, and instability compared to the calm demeanor of the less attractive Little Spike Buck. You see, humans and deer are not that different. The majority of the time when women look for a mate, they base it off of looks and first impressions. This is not the best way to choose a mate since they might have underlying issues such as being abusive, both verbally and physically or they may only treat their female companions with respect and dignity only when they want to breed or have sex. This leads to issues of passing on the not so perfect DNA to their offspring and allowing the diseases of mental illness to be passed down to their kids/fawns. The opposite can be true of the Little Spike Buck or inferior male humans when being selected by a mate. The true men of the herd and of the race are often not the most attractive physically. If the opposite sex can overlook the outside appearances and look deep into the soul and mind of the man or buck, then the positive and healthy DNA can be spread. So often this is not the case. Just as a beautiful rose or food such as a pie or meal looks flawless, the person selecting them will be more attracted to them as opposed to a messy looking plate of food or a less eye-appealing pie, rose or meal. This is nature in a nutshell. The dominant Big Rack Buck often loses out during the hunting season as their life span during hunting season is reduced or stopped completely since the larger bucks often get shot because their antlers are more attractive and better looking than the "inferior" Little Spike Buck. The Little Spike Buck often gets passed over by the hunters and gets to live another season. He may or may not ever get a bigger rack, so this "inferior" rack can be a blessing in disguise. With humans, this means that the less desirable male species can mature for a lot longer before getting a mate. This allows him to grow and mature before raising offspring and settling down. This also allows him to have more free time bonding with others and learning the "right way" of doing things and sharpening his skills in every arena of manhood.

Why is it so important for a man to find a mate? The scientific proposed opinion is that the man must pass on his DNA to his offspring and multiply. This is science's explanation. Is this the truth? Is this what we are supposed to believe, just as owning a home and nice car or truck with a huge salary and an important title or rank? I think and believe that this is what people of power and influence want us to believe. The real goal of achieving success is self-fulfillment, enrichment and happiness. This cannot be achieved thru wealth or material possessions. This is what we are taught to believe, and the majority of people are brainwashed, just like the hunter with shooting the Big Rack Buck and letting the Little Spike Buck walk to see another day. Just as the larger buck has no chance at living during hunting season, the same applies to not being able to live a happy life if you are the human striving for that big house, wife and kids, expensive car or truck and stressful life chasing financial success of having that dream job with a huge salary. Just as the token Big Rack Buck with a huge rack and supposedly dominant behavior gets all the doe, the man version of the Big Rack Buck also gets all the dough....in terms of money and wealth.

If you take a moment of all the Professionals with the title MD or PhD, or JD, or any other professional who is successful, they most likely have a certain look like the Big Rack Buck and gain success in part due to these attractive looks. It is human and animal nature to favor the more attractive. I have seen this first hand as you have too, but never really given it any thought or a lot of attention. This world is just like the deer woods.... full of resources for everyone but only the select few get the rewards for their attempt at living a fruitful life. Just like the doe that is more attracted to the hormone-filled and larger racked buck, the human female is more prone to be attracted to the handsome, muscular, wealthy or successful male. The deer that gets hunted more often is similar to the human male in his struggle to manage all this success. Sometimes it all falls apart just as the Big Rack Buck and he cannot fulfill all the expectations or goals of his so called "successful" life. What I am getting at is the so called "American Dream" is a myth. It is better to be the Little Spike Buck and live a quaint life of simplicity, repetitiveness and a life of the basics. This is how we should be living our lives.... with simplicity and more free time, down time and good times. Being the buck with the biggest antlers versus the buck with the little antlers both have their benefits. The bigger antlered bucks get first dibs on breeding the does in the herd and the little buck might get to breed and is not targeted during hunts and survives to live for another year. As any hunter brags about shooting the huge buck, a future wife brags about how sexy her boyfriend is to her friends. This is nature. It might not be fair or correct, but it is what it is. This is the modern-day tragedy of how vain and egotistical people are in today's world.

THE FISH IN THE POND

What is a Fisherman and why do they fish you may ask? A Fisherman is the oldest profession for men. It is a profession that can be hard work, fun and rewarding especially when the Fisherman can provide food for his family or a plethora of people. A Fisherman knows his environment and when to fish, where to fish and what to use as bait to catch the desired fish. This is a very well thought out process and is learned over the years of a Fisherman's experiences of successes and of failures. How do fisherman decide which fish to keep and which fish to throw back? It will primarily depend on size, maturity, sex and species and also Fishing Regulations unless you are on private property… but most fish that are caught and sought after are the larger fish. The experienced Fisherman will generally know which species he or she is going after, unless it is in the ocean or any salty body of water. You may use the same type of bait and catch a wide variety of fish in the ocean. In fresh water, you may target your fish species to be caught by using different types of bait also, but most of the time you will generally catch the same species when using the same baits. For example, if you are fishing a submerged brush pile and are using jigs or live minnows, you are most likely to catch perch or crappie and an occasional bass, which is rare. When drift fishing in deeper water and using live shad, you may catch striped bass or large catfish. When using shrimp in fresh water, you may catch catfish or a good eating fish, the gasper goo. You may also use liver or stink bait to catch catfish.

Most of the time, a Fisherman knows that the smaller fish and smaller fish of a desired species have more flavor and are easier to prepare. The fish are very smart and get smarter as they age. This implies that fish are adaptive and can use their minds well in making the right decision or choice when being targeted with artificial, or live baits such as crayfish, worms or insects, minnows, small perch and artificial lures like spinner baits or crankbaits. Baits such as dough stink bait, worms, jigs, spoons or flies may also be used.

Humans are also like fish being caught. They are fooled into thinking that the American Dream is a life filled with beautiful wives and handsome husbands, expensive clothes and cars or gigantic homes accompanied with huge salaries or a big title in their jobs such as MD, JD, PhD., MBA, etcetera. We are baited with all the glamour, riches, titles and power in relation to money and all the supposed things that it offers us. The bait is given to us all as children when we read comics, watch movies or other media, by social media and just talking to others about how to become successful. A really successful fisherman is happy with catching a smaller fish filled with flavor and when caught on light tackle and line, a great fight and very rewarding. The smaller fish not only taste better but are easier to clean, prepare and cook. This epitomizes the fact that making a decent living, having a decent home and a low stress life is better than being the big fish, not to mention a longer life-span, since most people who are novice fisherman will just throw you back. The more experienced or Professional Fisherman will be the minority and know that the smaller fish is way better than trying to catch and keep larger fish from the pond we all call modern day society. If you look at it from a Fisherman's perspective and see that the bigger the fish, it will most likely fit the size of a keeper and will go towards the creel limit for the day. This "keeper" fish cost the Fisherman time, money and energy and will bring the Fisherman some hard-earned money after he guts, scales and cleans the fish or alternatively, fillets both sides with a razor-sharp fillet knife after the fish has been iced for a period of time from the boat to the consumer. With most commercially farmed or caught fish, in most cases, the fish are frozen over 5 times before the consumer fry's, bakes, broils, grills or smokes the fish for their meal. If you are like me, you would prefer to have fresh fish, or in human terms, instant gratification. In relation to fishing, we often freeze our emotions multiple times before digging in and releasing them to our mates, partners, friends and other family members. With fresh caught fish/releasing emotional stressors immediately, the meal/relationship remains valued and consistently positive and healthy. If you look at it like this, we are all fisherman, with or without nets, poles, rods, spears, arrows, jugs or lines. We put our boats in the water/face society on a regular basis, catch our bait/make relationships, bait our hooks/maintain the love in our relationships, catch or catch and release our fish that we hook/either stay and maintain a healthy relationship or we end the relationship/s. As a Fisherman, we have all kinds of ways to catch fish and attract them with our baits and lures. This is similar to how people are attracted to one another. They base most of their attractiveness on visual looks and barely ever off of intellectual capacity. Often the potential mate is the one that is the most physically sexy not intellectually. This is not the same way in fish. Fish go after the opposite sex due to which mate will provide the most suitable offspring, based off of mentation, hormones, size and acceptability of the mate. Often, the looks fade over time and so does the love or attraction, unless there is something or some things more tangible that allows the partner of the relationship to benefit or be glad that they are in the relationship. True love is based off of unconditional feelings and thoughts related to the other person in the relationship. This is exactly why so many marriages fail.... because they are fishing for keepers/looking only at the trivial things that do not matter and do not value everything that the other person has to offer.... basing love on vanity and other not so important factors like title, power, position, salary, success or even looks. If we want to have happy and fulfilling relationships and eventually marriage, we must think outside of the fishing net and see the real keepers as the smaller fish that are in more abundance than their larger counterparts. If more people would be true fisherman and see all the good in the common, then we would have a merrier and brighter society filled with happier people and longer lasting relationships. When you fish again, try on for size the fight of a lifetime in a less large fish and take note in its intellectual beauty and proper-manner pageantry and you will be amazed at how happy you will be by giving the "throw-back" or catch and release fish a chance and of the benefits all the rewards and happiness that you have been missing by only focusing on the keeper/larger fish.

That's Big Game for a Little Kid...
Kid with a Pellet Rifle

ADVENTURES OF HUNTING THE FARM AND WOODS NEAR THE FAMILY HOME WITH .22 CALIBER BENJAMIN PELLET GUNS AND OTHER WEAPONS THAT WOULD DO THE JOB.

Chapter one:
DUCKS

As a Teenager, I was allowed to shoot the shotguns with someone else or preferably an adult…otherwise it was just my Benjamin Sheridan .22 Caliber Pellet Rifle. So, I called the brothers and we met up at our secret location and talked about our day, yes, this socialization is like therapy and we always felt better after venting for a few. The younger more tech savvy generation does not have this therapy and thus more school shootings and suicides and crime among the youth…compared to the Baby Boomers Kids generation.

It was November and in the beginning of deer season in Texas. We had a little three seat Chevy Luv four-wheel drive truck that was inherited to Joe from his father Larry. We would take two corded spotlights since every now and then the bulb burns up from constant use or it gets rain drops on it while it is hot and the glass cracks. We would spotlight at the ranch for rabbits and raccoons mainly. This was where we honed our skill on long distance shots of over 60 yards at night. I guess this is why my brothers and I have qualified on every available weapon system for use in combat situations. We used these hunting accuracy techniques to shoot ducks.

The mallards always nested here at the Snake Tank near my moms and dads…as you know, it had many a snake shot here. Today we spent working at our parent's homes, splitting firewood and living the farm life…because we did have money to drive to a remote location, cut down trees with axes then cut into smaller more manageable pieces then split the wood when it was dryer. We did this because we could not afford the gas and heat bill. Now I am thankful when we can afford to run the A.C. Or Heater.

The mallards would come in right before sunset. We made out primitive but affective reed, grass and cattail woven together duck blinds.

We waited and just like clockwork, the mallards came in by the dozens....I've never seen so many ducks in this pond, they must have been recruiting so that the odds of them living would be in their favor...little did they know I am an expert at poker and smoked 2 ducks and Joe and Carl shot one apiece. There is no telling how many we could have shot if I had no.2 steel shot and take the tube out have 5 shots at the ducks right before they land in the water.

And I forgot to tell you, we acted just like the retrievers do when it is time to recover the birds. We would strip to undies and wade thru the damn near freezing water then get the birds...but the good thing is that whoever did not get into their undies had to process ALL the birds while the other two would drink fruit punch Kool-Aid. I shot two Mallards. One was a drake and the other a hen. Back then, Taxidermy fees were out of my price range. So thus, I have no mounts of when I was younger, except my first buck...which I made payments on for almost a year...I still see it mounted in my room and remember that hunt and all that went into preparation and finalization of the hunt.

The way I shot two ducks is that I shot the mate of the other duck. I then shoot the partner and blam, two ducks...as opposed to the Brothers two ducks combined. I fetched the birds and we went to my house to chill and clean or bounty. My dad wanted us to cook the duck breast over pecan wood and have the breasts smoked and cooked medium-medium rare. We had garden fresh German Potatoes and Caramelized purple onion and steamed spinach and green beans and homemade biscuits and cream gravy. This was our first taste of killing big game with pellet rifles before this was popular with all these pneumatic and one pump air rifles.

Chapter two:
QUAIL

When I was fifteen, I shot my first quail.... native quail.... not raised and released into the wild. I miss those times during the evening of the quail....shoo sheet....shoo sheet....shoo sheet....just having an audio disco in your head. The other outdoorsy people would agree to have that sound of individualistic chirps and the people would give all the money in the world to regain their original quail habitat that was lost over the years and re-establish wild quail populations and eventually have managed habitat and a population sustainable for hunting with regulation of course.

I shot my first quail, a bobwhite in the woods near the airport....it was huge compared to the robin shot earlier that season. I shot it as it was perched on a yaupon limb in the thicket...I took aim and nailed her in the head without wasting any meat....I even saved the gizzards and hearts and still do to this day, even at age 42....talk about some excellent dirty Cajun Rice....it is so much better with real fresh livers and hearts. I love it...yes, my first name is French. No, Not Totino, but Beau. Totino is a book pen name so that people would not recognize my identity. Back to the story of the quail...I shot this one and put her into my backpack then walked the brush-laden fence-line and shot a few mourning dove, which were plentiful back then, not now, however more dove but most of them white wings. I had 5 birds to clean and cook...we ate good that night, fried quail, fried dove and freshly made dirty rice. That's my first quail experience...and shot with a pellet rifle. I have many other quail adventures of quail hunting in my lifetime. I will save those Adventures of Totino Ramen for another book or story.

Chapter three:
RABBITS

I actually saw and tasted my first fricassee when I was very young. You see, my mom drove a Citation, no, not a Cessna Citation that is my dream jet and way over my humble salary each month, but maybe one day, rather a Cessna Citation mini compact car. It sat so low to the ground and had about 4 inches of clearance and was perfect for running over dinner. My mom would make everything a game for us boys and this was one of them.... road hunting before it was popular...is it popular? not yet, but after people read this story then they will join in.

I had a Crossman .177 caliber pellet rifle and a daisy bb gun, which is mainly just for looks and can barely penetrate a coke can...unlike the .177 caliber pellet rifle, which if you are close enough to your game of choice, you can kill an animal up to a raccoon in size or as tough as a squirrel in tenacity, then it would be a clean death for that animal.

I would always take my Crossman .177 rifle when I went to work cattle with my dad and two brothers. I usually didn't shoot anything except turtles but that is still fun and honed my marksmanship skills. I did shoot my first rabbit from the back of a moving truck while checking cattle and throwing out range cubes. It was Spring time...I had my rifle set and loaded and took an amazing shot at a running Cottontail rabbit which we ate for dinner that night since we did not have anything else in the fridge or freezer for a meal. I remember this hunt since it was my 14th Birthday and we had smoked rabbit and corn bread for my birthday meal of choice. Once a Country Boy, Always a Country Boy! I shot many a rabbit with a .22 Long rifle all throughout High School and College years. I prefer rabbit hunting over raccoon hunting since you can actually eat rabbit without having to be a gourmet and experienced BBQ chef that know how to process, marinate and slowly baste as you roast that coon. I have done this twice in in my 42 years of life and it tastes like brisket, but a little gamey. More to come about raccoons.

THAT'S BIG GAME FOR A LITTLE KID... KID WITH A PELLET RIFLE

This chapter on Rabbits is closed for now. No...rabbits do have a lot of babies, but the mortality is so high that the majority of the family does not live to breed. So, in areas like where I am from, there are not that many coyotes since they all get shot during deer season. This makes the food chain stop at the rabbit. This means that the survival rates of the offspring are at or almost 100%. This is a good excuse to not go drinking with the other kids and to get a hand-me-down .22 with a scope that is older than you and spotlight on Friday and Saturday Nights until way past our bed time but not past our curfew since our parents knew we were good kids and at most we would dip snuff or chew tobacco like Red Man or Levi Garrett---my all-time favorite chew, but it had to be the plug...and we would all smoke swisher sweets...as if we were hot shots. We would rotate hunting spots, cause we had five spots to hunt that were over 100 acres each, some over 1,000 acres each. We never got stuck...we never drank beer, we never stole, we never lied, we never cheated...we shot small game and fed a lot of people, to include my family and the other poor families in the area that we could feed. I would guess that on average each hunt we would get 5 animals in the back of the truck...whether it be rabbits or raccoons we shot and cleaned and froze or gave away to the other poor people. We hunted in the winter months more than the Spring or Summer, but we did our best in the fall/a little cold part of the season. It. Is still when I have the most hunting success. I will say that with our Benjamin Sheridan .22 cal. Pellet rifles and our fathers' hand-me-down .22 Long Rifle with 15 plus 1 round capacity...so much easier than a Pellet Rifle, but you know what....it was more fun and challenging to kill the same animal with a .22 caliber pellet rifle as opposed to the semi-automatic 16 round .22 rifle! If you made a poor shot with the Benjamin, say at over 50 yards, open sight also, so every once in a while we would wound a rabbit, but you know how we solved this problem, driving closer to the rabbits or use the .22 Long Rifles instead, and use the pellet rifles at 30 yards or closer. So, after that point on, we had no wounded rabbits that needed to be specially cleaned and specially handled, since we don't wear gloves when hunting, only when skinning and gutting, and you could get blood or feces on you out in the field. Supposedly rabbits carry the fleas that carry bubonic plague…this is a myth…like saying Armadillos in Texas can cause Leprosy! This is also a myth. Yes, there is a difference between South American Armadillos and Armadillos in the United States and Mexico. There are Nine Banded and Seven Banded Armadillos respectively, but I am not sure why except Geographic Isolation and Modification of genetic code over a long period of time.

Chapter four:
SQUIRRELLS

As a ten-year old child and having possessed bb guns previous in life, I had two best friends that were country neighbors and they owned Benjamin Sheridan .22 caliber pellet rifles. I had a Daisy bb gun/.177 caliber pellet rifle and I would hunt with the Benjamin Brothers for multiple species. They would always kill what they shot and what I shot would have feathers flying everywhere and no kills. I picked pecans, I picked dewberries, and I cut a lot of grass with a real old school push mower for months before I had over a hundred dollars cash. This was just enough money to buy a Benjamin of my own at Academy, but also some targets and some pellets. I preferred the dome pellets back then…now for small game I prefer the domed pellets.

Actually, I just took my .300 WIN MAG scope, yes, the scope I took 6 boxes to zero at 200 yards, and I put that scope on my deceased fathers .22 Remington 550-1 and I sighted it in at 100 yards, bullet on bullet…and yes, back to my point, this is a great varmint exterminator, especially for squirrels that you want to put with dumplings and vegetables…and make squirrel and dumplings. Well, back to the story…it was around Christmas time, which means duck migrating to the Southern States for wintering…just like the old timers come from upstate and fly to their homes in Florida….they are smart but it is called wintering nonetheless…and Floridians calling them SNOWBIRDS, and I learned that a lot of SNOWBIRDS come to Florida to winter and over half of them are recovering or struggling alcoholics. I went since I was in a treatment facility for the 10% of men that get sexually assaulted by another man or multiple men. I was struggling to hold it together when the other victors of victimology told their stories and how they would cry and we all would cry….it was kind of like exposure therapy verbally and visibly with a real breathing human being. I kept my shit together towards the end of the program after three months of processing and having barely enough time to get ripped at the gym and a few trips to the Beaches in the surrounding area of Bay Pines, Florida. We had all been struggling for a while…unfortunately we kind of all lost touch or life…Cody, he killed himself just a few months after Bay Pines, and Greg is pissed at me for telling him that I was going to get a huge check for oil and gas royalties….I was testing him, he did not ask for money, and he never spoke of it…but I think that he was struggling emotionally or financially and got jealous in a good way. I was like a brother for Cody and Greg. Cody was really traumatized of being in an Airborne Unit and getting raped by a Senior Non-Commissioned Officers. Once when I told my story about being drugged just a week before coming home from a two-year long hardship tour as an Airborne Ranger and Air Assault Infantry Officer. I spoke of getting drugged and knowing of at least 5 of the guys who were Non-Commissioned Officers and Also Fellow Officers. Once they found out that being sexually assaulted as a TOUGH GUY and BILLY BAD-ASS and am in the same program as they were in. We were best of friends and would eat every meal, take every pass, grill together, watch movies together and lift weights together…and a little guitar playing and hitting the salvia divonorum when it was legal in Florida then outlawed…it was like weed, except it made everything look like cartoons. I could not help but laugh my ass off for over ten minutes straight.

I left the house after finishing my chores and headed to meet up after calling ####-8#0-##### to see if the brothers would want to hunt

THE DEER IN THE WOODS AND THE FISH IN THE POND

squirrels in the woods behind the airport. The feeling was that they were tired of sitting on the ground for squirrels that they would never eat or even much less clean. I convinced them that if we saw a rabbit or a snake that they had first shots at the target. I needed some meat to feed my family of five, yes, I was a teenager and had the burden of putting food on the table on a regular basis…so I needed two squirrels to feed 5 people, which basically means two pieces of meat per person if you butcher the squirrel into 10 pieces and freeze the other half so that you don't have to jack with the greasy and smelly cut up fat as hell full of steroid bagged discount chicken. This is why America is OBESE and ought to shape. Squirrel, especially fresh and not frozen red fox squirrels and bled, skinned, saving the hides for making something cool after they were properly tanned, and the squirrel meat seasoned and sautéed in buttermilk or Italian dressing…for at least an hour then pan fried in butter in a heavy duty iron skillet until browned on all sides, then. Add water, potatoes, onions and carrots and celery then simmer for an hour on medium-low heat…just to keep it warm and it could be served with cornbread or flour tortillas or Kings Hawaiian Rolls… the best, but expensive…and totally worth it. We all met up 15 minutes later at our secret end of the world spot to link up and survive the mass destruction with pellet rifles, pellets, knives, and fishing gear for a lifetime and the knowledge learned in life to actually know what survivalists know. Carl had his dads pellet rifle from the early 60's and this was 1993, and the damn thing still had power and distance with every shot and Joe had a pellet rifle of the same Benjamin and Sheridan specs and was also a .22 caliber and then you have me…Totino Ramen, with a straight out of the box Benjamin Sheridan rifle and a cool pellet bag that I stored my 200 pellets. Joe and I sighted it in at our secret spot and it took about 10 pumps for 10 good shots, which is 100 pumps total… of the last three shots bullet on bullet…yes I said that…that's as lit as bullet on bullet…not only accurate, but also precise. We all had strong grips and forearms on both arms after hunting all the time with those pump up air rifles when we were kids. Carl was sitting by his old faithful Oak tree with acorns all at the base and some chewed

THAT'S BIG GAME FOR A LITTLE KID... KID WITH A PELLET RIFLE

up acorn shells all scattered into a neat little pile of sorts, and he always saw or shot a squirrel at this spot...just like my spots at the lake that are guaranteed to catch at least a couple of fish....and I sat 30 feet to the south, or deeper into the squirrel woods and I was there for five minutes and I smoked a female red fox squirrel at about 35 yards. I bled it and bagged it and was excited that since I needed two for supper and I already had one. Then I heard a shot, it was Carl...he dropped one with his dad's old pellet rifle and it hit the ground with a thud. We bled it and Joe, and I went to see if there were any turtles or snakes to be shot by the secret pond location.... Called the Big Bass Tank. Totino, or myself rather, had to get home to finish processing the freshly harvested meat and have it ready for supper...it was a Friday night so we went to bed later and it was already 5:30 p.m. so I needed enough time to have supper cooked and served at an appropriate hour to where we are not totally starving. We shot at a few turtles because everyone knows that turtles eat fish...well...that's what the urban legend is, but not all turtles eat fish...surprise...surprise.... the eat vegetation. SO, I wonder how many harmless turtles we shot at our favorite fishing holes. It took me about five minutes to skin, gut and process each squirrel and then the easy part...margination of the meat with my secret ingredients of Italian dressing or buttermilk then season with Zataran's or Slap Ya' Mama Cajun style seasonings which were added after the marinade/margination then have that iron skillet hot and ready for the squirrel meat, soaking in all that butter which will eventually be made into cream gravy for the biscuits that we are going to make for an accompaniment to this fine dinner. We usually had company for dinner when we were young...I did not know until 25 years later that my mom was feeding all the neighbors poor kids when we had more than enough to eat or even if we had little to eat... we still had a meal...even if it were beans and no cornbread or chili with crackers...the crackers were usually stale, but out of respect to your family, especially your mom and dad, you kept it to yourself since you knew they were doing their best to be good providers. We usually ate squirrel either fried then stewed, fried then dumplings, fried then eaten...LOL then grilled over direct heat and with pecan wood to add smoky flavor component. Since we had two squirrels that evening, makes it enough to give everyone two pieces of meat and a helping of rice or potatoes. I was the honorary server, as I was most every other meal...this just means that I ate less since the food was almost gone since there was so little food to go around...I gave my mom a hind leg and a tenderloin, same for my dad, and everyone else just got whatever they damn well pleased and I couldn't keep track...it was like wolves on a two week unsuccessful hunt then they run across a dead elk.... that they ate in like 15 minutes, bones and all. I ended up with only one front quarter and a few vegetables...and I was full after that. I usually eat all the things that I don't like first and then eat what I do like last so that the meal ends on a positive tone/note. At least all the guests got two pieces of squirrel to go with the dumplings and other sides. It really was a meal fit for a king at any age...and still to this day hunt and fish to provide for my family and close friends.

Chapter five:
SNAKES

I saw my first up close and personal snake when the neighbor had killed a 6-foot chicken snake. I was, maybe, five years old. The snake was getting into his coop first thing in the morning and evening as the sun was setting each day. Mr. Edgar knew this since he left eggs in the morning and eggs in the evening to bait the snake and feed it its last rights meal. Mr. Edgar waited outside the coop with a 2x4 and a machete. He killed the snake and hung it on the fence so that it would produce rain and/or keep other snakes away...or this is what we were taught. There are a lot of things we are taught and apply towards every-day living and even complicated business and personal decisions. Like a penny saved is a penny earned, or you will have 7 years of bad luck for breaking a mirror, or the cats got your tongue. I actually saw my first real live rattlesnake on our farm out in the sticks. It was a Timber Rattler or Kane

Break Snake. I also shot it with my Benjamin .22 Caliber pellet rifle. It was very easy to clean and cut into three-inch strips and fried like fish or chicken and it was amazing and tasted like frog legs…no…not like chicken…actually to tell you the truth, it tasted like rattlesnake!

I was not scared of the dead snake on the neighbor's fence. I was actually rather intrigued by the scales on its skin and wanted to skin a snake to hang on my wall with my raccoon skin, rabbit skin, and squirrel skins. My mom was and is still cool about me hanging stuff like that in my bedroom. Yes, I am Totino Ramen and I'm 42 and single. I don't have much, but what I have is enough. I saw water snakes at the Airport tank that my Great Uncle Hap had stocked with perch and catfish. I saw a few water snakes there when I was younger and shot a few every summer with the brothers and all of us sporting .22 Caliber Benjamin Pellet Guns. One time, as my faithful dog, Rocky, was basking in the sun on a sandy beach on the bank, there was a real water moccasin swimming full speed ahead on top of the water headed directly to Rocky who was fast asleep. I was actually fishing that day and hardly ever bring my rifle, but this day I did. I instinctively grabbed and shouldered my rifle and took one magical shot that hit the snake in its back, paralyzing it and it was shot again in the head. I attribute my good shot placement with how the snake was in an S-shape on top off the water. I think that made things easier. I still think that is one of my greatest shots in my life and will be talked about after I'm gone.

Chapter six:
TURTLES

I saw my first turtle crossing the road when I was only 4. caught several varieties while driving country roads, most notable a 35-pound Alligator Snapping Turtle and a 20-pound Softshell Turtle. This was way before times of having a digital camera or a smart-phone and I took the turtles home to show off before releasing them back to where I found them. Usually after a heavy rain, the water turtles will move to another pond, river or creek. I attribute this to them being able to have fresh rain water in puddles when or after it rains.

My first turtle was a male Box Turtle with those oh so lovely orange markings. There's a story behind this also. We were on a road trip to get roped into buying a time-share property. We were promised a large screen color T.V. as if the younger generation would know about black and white T.V., since this was all that the Ramen family could afford. We never did get that T.V. from the time-share scam, but while we were driving, as usual, all three of us boys are playing I Spy games or just looking at nature and counting and counting. I usually had the best eyesight, so I saw the box turtle from a distance. I told my dad who was driving our Citation, to let us pick it up and take it home. He was a good man too, and he agreed. This is my favorite tortoise that I have ever had as a pet, and for that matter, the only tortoise I've had for a pet. Now, about the Alligator Snapping Turtle. I was once again, riding shotgun in my dad's Chevy Luv diesel pickup truck. We were rounding a corner on the gravel, now paved, road and my dad hit the brakes. He was a nature lover and would always try and prevent hitting animals if he had a choice. After hitting the brakes, he said, "Turtle!". I had never seen an Alligator Snapping Turtle before. I picked up the turtle and gently placed him on the closed bed of the truck. We only had a mile to go from the creek to our house. Once I got home with my new turtle pet…I went inside the house to get a piece of sandwich bread to feed to the turtle, cause all novice animal lovers will think that the animal needs food and water, like a prisoner in a jail cell. SO..I went inside, got two pieces of bread and proceeded to try and feed the new dinosaur of a turtle. I placed the bread right by his beak/mouth and he damn near ate the whole piece of bread along with my right thumb. Being the Boy Scout I was, I ALWAYS had a pocket knife on me. All my brothers were and still are like that. I reached into my right pocket with my left hand…pulled out the knife, opened it, and then stabbed the turtle in the leg with it and it let go. I stabbed it with the corkscrew on my imitation Swiss Army Knife. It was treated with antibiotic cream and then after showing everyone in my family the turtle, we took it back to the same place that we found it and released it back into the wild. These are only a sample of turtle stories that Totino has experienced in his short life and younger days.

Chapter seven:

RACCOONS/AND WHAT IN THE WORLD IS THAT? OH MAN, THAT'S A RING-TAILED CAT

When I was a kid, at age 3, I was as patient and calm as can be and I was not like the kid that asked "Who..What…When….Where…..Why?". I loved wild animals and nature, so I got to go on all kinds of supervised hunts until I was 13 and hunted WTD-White Tailed Deer. Back to the Raccoon stories. My dad and a bunch of his friends and employees would go raccoon/coon hunting once a month for 3 months during winter, one to shoot, two to kill, three to eat and four to sell…sell the tanned hides. So, I got to retrieve all the dead coons, even the ones laying in between two branches of a tree, and I was the only Monkey that could climb that high and on such small limbs. I only had to do this five or six times… in my lifetime. Generally, when you make a clean head shot on a coon, it 9 times out of 10 will fall to the ground. I did get to go coon hunting with the brothers father and we were on our property and we hit the mother lode of raccoons in one tree…over 20 raccoons in one tree… you see, we had two .22 Benjamins and 2 .22 Remington rifles and we had to shoot some of the coons in the head again due to not lethal shot placement prior to them hitting the ground…so we shot 15 rounds out of the .22 Remington's and then shot a few more with the .22 Caliber Benjamin Air Rifles. I wish that whoever retrieved the coons like the birds would not have to clean the coons, but this did not exist, and since they drove their truck with their gas and guns and ammo, I had the clean all of the over 20 in number raccoons. I was good at sharpening knives, so I always carried and always used a razor-sharp knife. It took maybe 30 seconds per coon to gut, and I used the Ford Assembly line method, gutting then skinning then portioning into what is cooked whole, fried, baked, or BBQed. It was also the final step to feed the poor in the area. I skinned each coon in about 2 minutes flat. I had just enough room in our family freezer to put 10 portioned raccoon pieces and 2 whole raccoons for cooking whole. We froze them and we gave the rest to our poor neighbors. All in all, three coolers filled with one bag of ice and the rest either filled with coon pieces/quarters and whole raccoons. They were so appreciative and thankful of the blessing of all the fresh meat. I felt good about myself and was more confident that hunting is a sport and a way of life. It sure did provide many a meal for my family and so many other poor families in our area. I continue to hunt, and fish and I always act ethically and respectfully of the Hunt and of the Harvest. One time, we hunted late into the night/early morning…cause we told our parents we were going camping…they knew that we were good kids so we pretty much got away with anything legal, and some-times not so legal, like shooting a deer at night so we could have meat for the winter. We had to do it at night since we knew that if we got caught, we could at least say that we thought it was a coyote and didn't want to waste the meat. We hunted until the sun was about to come up…then out of nowhere we saw a raccoon at about 5oo yards away in a tree…I caught it in the spotlight and held the light true for a while then my arm would get tired and it did get tired so I switched hands and then we lost the glowing eyes in or light. We waited a while then shined the light to a neighboring tree and there was the same raccoon that we had seen earlier….it looked like he had a yearling coon with him….we shot them both and when I went to retrieve our bounty, I noticed one small problem…one was a fat raccoon and the other one looked like a large squirrel with rings on its tail like a raccoon. We had never seen one before, so Ryan,

My best friend at the time kept it frozen until he had enough money to have it mounted…I think he still has that mount and is very proud of it. It was also, since you are wondering, a Ring-Tailed Cat.

Chapter eight:
SKUNKS

On occurrence several spotlighting Friday Night Adventures would include shooting 2 huge bobcats, yes, we made carpets out of the hides, and furthermore the bobcats were killing this guy's chickens that he depended on for his survival, since he sold the eggs at the market every day. We also shot about a dozen Skunks, which yes, do carry more rabies than any other North American Mammal and in our area at that particular ranch, we saw about 50 different skunks. They would pop like a balloon when you hit them in the head with a .22 hornet or .22 magnum or .17 HMR rifle or 22.250 or 25.06 high powered rifle. I also found out that the bad smell coming from skunks is their urine and it is never wasted unless there is a life-threatening situation or in self-defense or as a warning to their aggressor or potential aggressor. Skunks pelts are highly sought after, for my neighbor that is, and can go for up to $200.00 for each one. So, 10 skunks could potentially bring $2,000.00. That's a lot of money for high school kids. This meant that we could get the c.b. radios in our jeeps, cd players in our jeeps, and good off-road tires and a winch mounted to the front. I think that jeeps have the ultimate poor man's four wheel drive, as opposed to the Land Rover Defender series or the Range Rover Sport that outfitted with all-terrain tires and a 3 inch lift, then the Jeep Wranglers and definitely the Jeep Cherokee's will have a tough time out-performing these Miraculous off road beasts. I'm an American, so I will stick with Jeep as my primary and maybe one day I will also get a Defender 90 with everything needed and then some. With a little bit of money and time, you could outfit a Jeep to the same specifications as a Defender or Range Rover Sport that is tricked out.

THE DEER IN THE WOODS AND THE FISH IN THE POND

Chapter nine:
ARMADILLO

When we would drive on long road trips, or even short trips, my eyes were scanning for wildlife.... preferably alive, but dead would have worked too. On many occasions I would see a lot of dead animals, but most of the time I would not see anything. What irked me the most was that there was a lot of dead armadillos, our state mammal, lying lifeless on the side of the road. I never saw an armadillo while hunting. One time while I was scouting our ranch, as a young boy, I carried a .22 pellet rifle in case I saw any rattlesnakes or needed to shoot anything else. I was walking the woodline and scanning for life. After walking for about five minutes and getting closer to the pond and further away from the creek, in the distance, about 50 yards away, I spotted something gray, digging a hole under an old oak tree, and yes, it was an armadillo. I walked practically right up to it before it could sense that I was there. I know that they had excellent hearing but poor vision, so I aimed at its head and squeezed the trigger. It was a hefty male and had that unusual Armadillo smell to it. I gutted it and put it in my backpack and decided to head back to the truck. I took the freshly killed armadillo to my dad's worker, Perry and he cleaned it and actually put it in the fridge for cooking/BBQing that weekend. He invited me since he said it tasted good. I agreed and showed up there hesitant to try BBQed armadillo. At first, I took a small bite, and realized that it was so flavorful, like ribs and I ate quite a bit more. I never shot another armadillo since that particular hunt, but If I do, I am going to BBQ it and just tell everyone that it is ribs and then after they devour it, I will tell them the truth.

Chapter ten:
PIGEONS

As a young hunter and avid outdoorsman, I shot many a pigeon at my dad's feed store in town. They were not as easy to shoot and kill as you would think. I shot a few and feathers went everywhere only to have those pigeons fly higher into the rafters of the feed mill where it was hard for me to take a second shot and take them out for good. In these cases, I would take a head shot and that would do the trick. I shot probably 4-5 each time I went hunting at the feed mill. This was just enough for us to all eat one pigeon each in my family. I think that pigeon tastes a lot like dove or duck. We would generally cook them over a bed of coals on the BBQ pit and season them with salt, pepper and baste them with lemon juice and melted butter for added flavor. I think that BBQ pigeon was my favorite wild game meal. I only dreaded plucking all the birds of all their feathers. This was definitely a labor of love to say at the least. I shot the most and bagged the most pigeons with my old faithful .22 Benjamin pellet rifle. I did shoot a few with my Daisy .177 caliber pellet rifle. Did I mention that I saved up for an entire year to buy that .22 cal. Pellet rifle? Yes, I picked pecans, until my fingers were green, picked dewberries until my hands were purple and some of my grubby clothes turned purple. I remember getting a "Just Say No to drugs" t-shirt at school and I think I wore it almost every time my friends and I would go hunting in the back pasture/woods and when we would pick berries or pecans. I think that free t-shirt lasted over 9 years....yes, 9 years, cause I wore it for 4 years and then my little brother wore it for 4 years then a family friend wore it for a year or two...I am not 100% certain, but in any case, we wore the heck outta that shirt and got our monies worth out of it. It was full of holes and stained but it was a great shirt and could tell many a hunting and fishing story if it could talk. Well, back to the pigeon hunting. The best time to hunt pigeons was right before dark since they were headed to roost. This worked out for me since my dad had us working at the feed mill after school most days. We would do menial tasks that his workers would not do all the time, like sweeping, mopping, organizing and the like. I would love to finish early and hunt pigeons until dark. Eventually I would cheat and had a flashlight and would blind the birds in their roost and then smoke them with one shot only and then put them in my backpack so that I could clean them later and we could have a good meal. I did see a few rats in my years of hunting at the feed mill and shot them every time that I had the opportunity. I also shot a few mice too and did this on a regular basis until we had a resident stray cat, then two, then three then almost 10 stray cats. We would feed them of course and they would keep the rodent population down to a minimum or at zero. I sure do miss those days of sitting patiently by the feed pile in the mill and shoot my fill on pigeons. I miss it so much that I sit patiently each year for about 5-6 hunts, yet this time, for larger game such as squirrels and white-tailed deer. I hunt the deer with either a Marlin 30.30 or a Remington 30.06 and the squirrels with a .22 Remington or a .32 caliber Pedersoli Hawken's black powder rifle which is way more fun and challenging.

Chapter eleven:
POSSUMS

Possums are not the most sought-after species to hunt. They are the only Marsupial in the United States and they pretty much look like a huge rat. I am not sure why, but at one property that we hunted on we would always shoot two or three possums every time we spotlighted there. I did not ever eat one myself, well, maybe not, but I bet I did at my neighbors BBQ party one winter. It was the mystery meat and he kidded saying it was possum.... I ate it and it was ok...kind of' greasy and gamey but good enough to eat in a survival situation. I would clean all the possums that we shot and give the meat to the poor black family in the trailer home down the road. They were very appreciative and thankful so I would make it a point to bring them fresh meat that we shot every week or at a minimum every other week. Possums will play like they are dead and would be better shot in the head up close since a bad shot would make them play dead and then when you went to pick them up, they could all of a sudden come back to life and bite you with their razor-sharp teeth. This double tapping of the possum was necessary for our own protection. Initially when we were first starting out possum hunting with spotlights, one time we wounded a possum and it was apparently playing dead and we threw it onto the back of the truck. Ten minutes later, as I was on the back of the truck, I yelled, "STOP THE TRUCK" ..." STOP THE TRUCK"! The possum that we thought was dead came back to life and was attacking me. We stopped the truck and luckily, we had a .22 pellet rifle and smoked it with that instead of shooting it with a .22 long rifle and putting a hole in the truck. This was not uncommon to shoot an animal and it was placed on the back of the truck to only come back to life in the bed of the truck.... I attribute this to shock and is totally preventable if the animal was double tapped in the head. This is the only way to know for sure that the animal is shot with the least amount of pain and suffering. We did shoot probably a dozen possums over the course of 4 years of spotlighting almost every Friday night...and yes I did go to the college football games, skipping high school Friday Night Lights...I would go fishing in the morning of the Saturday games and would spend the rest of the day watching my favorite teams play good ole college football. I don't watch all the games now but do watch about 2-3 games each Saturday. This year as is every year is our year to win it all be the National Champions. I predict that we will play the University of Texas in the final game...yes...we will win the SEC and Texas will win the Big 12. I hope I'm right. We have not won a title since 1939....80 years ago.

Chapter twelve:

WHITE TAIL DEER

I first went deer hunting when I was only 5 years old.... I remember that hunt like it was recent. My dad let me read some hunting books/magazines the night before the hunt to get me in the hunting spirit. We had a farm about 15 minutes away and back then no one used feeders or food plots, so we hunted in box blinds in places where deer were known to go and eat or drink water. It was cold that morning but not as cold as it was when the cold front blew in. You see, we did not have apps for weather back then either. It got so darn cold that my dad and I went to look for something to keep me warm. I was wearing a long-sleeved shirt and wrangler jeans and cowboy boots. He was a survivalist and found a trash bag by the creek. He proceeded to cut two holes for arms to go thru and he stuffed the bag into my wranglers and stuffed it full of dried leaves. Sure enough, this made me warm and comfortable for the entire hunt. I distinctly remember him using his 30.06 Springfield bolt-action rifle. We sat for half the day and only saw squirrels. We still had fun and it was a great memory. My first deer I shot with my mom's 30.30 Marlin lever action. I actually shot two deer in the same hunt. The first group that I shot was four doe running at a slow pace at around 50 yards. I smoked the doe and then out of no-where a 6-point buck was crossing the barbed wire fence at 25 yards and I shot him while he was jumping, and I smoked him too. I was hunting with my big brother and little brother and a family friend. No one else shot anything and they all thought I shot myself since I shot twice. I laughed when they told me that as we tracked the two deer. I still have the picture of the doe that we skinned at my mom's house. Yes, my Mom taught me how to skin my first two deer. I have shot so many deer that I probably have over 100 harvested deer in my 35 years of white-tailed deer hunting. Now that we have something called management tags, I shoot at least 4 deer each season. I have also progressed to more difficult hunting like bow and arrow, crossbow and black powder in-line and Hawken's rifles also. I have only harvested 5 doe with bow and arrow/compound bow and one with crossbow and 3 with black powder....one with my .54 Davide Pedersoli Hawken's and one with my .32 caliber Davide Pedersoli Hawken's and 3 with my Traditions Buckmaster .50 cal. Inline and one with my Thompson Center .50 Cal. In line rifle, which needs to be re-sighted in before I hunt with it again since I dropped it when unloading my truck. I have planned on sighting all the rifles that I use before the season starts, but I never seem to have the time. I cannot wait until I am a millionaire or billionaire so I will have more time…LOL. That is one thing that we all have the same amount of…time…and it is up to us how we utilize it and enjoy it. I have learned that life is short, and it is imperative to use your time wisely.

Chapter thirteen:

DOVE---A MULTITUDE OF SHARPSHOOTING SKILLS BRO---WHITE-WING AT 80 YARDS BRO...WITHOUT MY AMMO---

Well, I saved the best for last, I guess. I probably have more dove kills than with any other rifle or shotgun. Every dove season the pasture next to my mom's and dad's house had hundreds of dove lining the powerline above the 100-acre field of dove weed or goat weed, which produces a seed that the dove cannot resist. In the past ten years, the white-wing dove has pretty much taken over and somehow diminished the mourning dove population. I recalled for years I would only limit out on my dove and they were all mourning dove. About 15 years ago the white-winged dove are more prevalent. They are now the majority and the mourning dove are the minority. I believe last season I only bagged four mourning dove our of over 100 dove, meaning that 96% of the dove were white-winged dove. In recent years I have also seen more ring-necked dove. I have never shot one since they generally fly really high and if I did shoot it would be a miracle to bag one of these dove. This year I am going to hunt with two shotguns...one loaded with no. 7.5-8 bird shot and the other shotgun loaded with steel shot...number 6 steel bb's flying fast enough with enough knock down power to smoke those high-flying white wings and elusive collard doves.... or ring-neck doves. I usually limit out the first few days and fest on dove breasts wrapped with bacon and jalapeno peppers and a little cream cheese...they are like the jalapeno poppers at Sonic Drive In but oh so much more flavorful and meaningful. I also will have like I have before, a .22 caliber pellet rifle by my side in case a dove flies and lands in a tree near my hunting spot. I will shoot them with the pellet rifle so that I don't shoot them with an expensive shotgun shell. I like to try my skills at marksmanship since I usually take head shots. I can accomplish this since there is a 3x9x 32 scope that is sighted in at 50 yards. I use dome pellets for this or hollow pointed pellets. Generally, every year I bag about 5-10 dove the whole season this way.

The way that I do my dove and prepare them is that right after they are shot and down on the ground, I pull their heads off and throw them in my hunting bucket. I shoot my limit then I clean them, saving the gizzards and hearts for Cajun dirty rice. I breast out the dove and cut the meat off the breast bone with a sharp fillet knife and keep them in a Ziplock bag and marinate them in Italian dressing with some beef BBQ seasoning. I marinate them for about 4-5 hours then prepare the grill for cooking the wrapped breasts. When I was a kid and my dad was still alive…he made me pluck the entire bird and keep the gizzards livers and hearts. It took me a long time to do this and it sucked. It would take about 4 minutes to pluck every feather off of the dove. I kept this tradition alive for many years after he passed away but changed my cleaning technique a few years ago when I realized that there was maybe a bite extra if cleaning the birds totally. I don't waste the dove remains after breasting them…I cook them for my hunting companion Ranger, and he loves grilled dove. I am glad that I use the whole bird… otherwise It would be wasteful and unethical. I have shot 40-60 dove every season for the last 10 years. I have a 12-gauge black powder shotgun that is a double barrel. I want to use it this year and shoot like they did 100 years ago and see how good I really am. I mastered the single shot, over and under, pump and semi-automatic shotguns…so this is my last shotgun to master hunting with. I love dove hunting since this was the first real game hunting that I did when I was so young and with my little and big brother and my mom and dad. It brings back so many good memories and makes me happy. Good luck to you if you hunt and be safe…no game animal is worth risking your life over. It is a sport and should be a challenge and fun if you allow it to be.

Excuse Me, Thank You, No Thank You, Yes Ma'am, Yes Sir, You're Welcome, I'm Sorry, I Apologize, Yes Please, and Forgive Me

"Treat everyone with LOVE, COMPASSION, RESPECT…IF IT WOULD HURT YOU THEN IT WILL HURT THEM…LISTEN MORE…BE HUMBLE AND KIND…ALL THE TIME…IT WILL ALLOW YOU INNER PEACE AND HAPPINESS."

Excuse me: Everyone in the world makes mistakes sometimes. It is appropriate to say excuse me in situations where you have passed gas accidentally or you have accidentally bumped into someone while shopping, walking or doing everyday things, or when you cut into line on accident since the other person looked like they were not actually in line. The simple phrase of "excuse me" can and will go a long way.

Thank you: It is always good to hear "thank you" from anyone and to anyone. This little phrase can open doors for you, and you will be blessed in the future by just saying this simple phrase. It is appropriate in almost any situation, from receiving a compliment, for being blessed by someone else with gifts, a good meal, a surprise party, a birthday warm wish, for doing a good deed and being recognized for it. "Thank you" should be used every day. If you are not sure of when it is appropriate to use thank you, use it anyway and it is sure to be appropriate.

No thank you: This is a good way to be polite and get out of a sticky situation. For example, it is imperative to use this term when you don't feel 100% comfortable with what the person is asking you to do. An example is when someone offers you a drink or to smoke a cigarette or anything of similar in nature. No thank you allows you to refuse falling into the "peer pressure" and allows you to be you. This is a good way to stand your ground and stand up for your beliefs without being rude in conjecture.

Yes Ma'am: Yes, Ma'am is a life saver for a young man or a young lady. This term can work wonders when a woman figure in your life asks you to do something. By saying a simple "Yes Ma'am" you are showing respect and acknowledging them in a proper manner. Yes, Ma'am can be used in a casual way also and in a formal way. Casually, by saying "Yes ma'am", you are showing the utmost respect to that individual and this is a way to be honorable and a lady or a gentleman in deed. Formally, with a friend or adult figure, "Yes Ma'am" is necessary to show a higher level of respect and honor and also works wonders when trying to convey utmost honor and respect. Saying "Yes Ma'am" on a regular basis will make it become habit and you will be known as the person who has good manners and is a lady or gentleman.

Yes Sir: Yes, Sir is a life saver for a young lady or young man. This phrase works wonders especially when you are unsure of what a man's name is. Just say Yes Sir and you are good to go. As a young adult this phrase is golden and shows that you are a respectful young man or young lady. It is even appropriate to use with your father, father figure, uncle or any adult man in your life. Saying "Yes Sir" on a regular basis will make it become habit and you will be known as the person who has good manners and is a gentleman or a lady.

You're Welcome". You're welcome and you're most welcome is definitive of being humble and kind at the same time and respectful in recognizing that you have done something of merit that deserves a remark. You can say you're welcome to someone who has told you thank you for some kind act of generosity or in deed that you have done for them to help them. An example would be like this…you have a young kid who opens the door at the grocery store for an elderly lady and she says, "Thank you son." You reply with "you're welcome" and that is the best way to be humble and kind while being respectful.

I'm sorry: I am sorry or I'm sorry is a good one to use when you know you have messed up and you really want to be apologetic and own up your mistake or flaw. I probably say I'm sorry a million times a day, more used than any other gesture or phrase. Don't use it like a question, so saying I'm sorry in a sarcastic way in no way will be a part of your language repertoire. Don't ever yell at someone and say… "I'm Sorry." Or Say it so soft that no one can hear you. And don't giggle when you say it either, otherwise you will lose all hope of getting an appropriate response. Saying "I'm sorry might not get you out of doing your taxes, but it has saved many a marriages and friendships…. what's a friend without "I'm Sorry." or "I love you."

I apologize: "I apologize" ... can be used in any conversation where you offend someone...or when you make a mistake and are sincere about your mistake and you want to put the person at ease when they know you are a sincere and genuine person. I apologize can also be used for gassy situations that do not take place at the pump with unleaded or biofuels....it is when you pass gas that is so smelly and foul that you have to actually apologize for and then pass another gas bomb in a few more minutes and apologize for this too...but this would not be sincere...rather skeptical since you are not sincere about your apology. Another good apology is when you apologize for not picking the phone up and then doing the same thing to the same exact person every day for the next few days.

Yes Please: "Yes Please" is the all-time "baby-boomer and older generation"...when they hear yes please at the ending of a sentence...or as the entire sentence itself.....one will be delighted to hear and the one saying these words will be delighted at the up and coming treat or reward every time following saying "Yes Please!"

Forgive me:" Forgive me! Go forgive yourself. Or forgive me please.... or Please forgive me.... if you are saying any or all of these then you might be in deep mud without a shovel...or worse yet.... with a baby spoon instead. If you say forgive me at just the right time...you might be forgiven a smidgen...but not more than that....it gives your spouse something to talk about for a while...until the next argument and then you are getting on your knees for forgiveness and crawling back to them like a worm in a bed of fire ants.

"I Did That for Lunch Money": A Rambling Yet Ordered Mess

A short story on stealing from parents pockets, friends change drawer, ashtray in friends vehicle, anyone you knew vehicle, washed and detailed airplanes, cut grass, raked leaves, picked berries, picked pecans, hauled hay, just to have enough money for school lunches. thank god our mother fed us a good breakfast, yes, good breakfast---even then, my mom was ahead of her time in regards to nutrition and health---then if we did not have a lunch, we definitely had a snack right after school----my favorite---the nutty bar, Butterfinger, and snickers---yes, these are my top three, only had about once a year since we were so poor, and we always had cereal of multiple kinds for adults and for kids….my favorite adult were raisin bran and bran flakes, then corn flakes with real sugar and back then there weren't any fancy granola cereals, or honey nut cheerios…we always had cereal cause momma would buy it in like 50 pound bags, right by the pet food aisle…yes, my brothers were pains in the rear sometimes, but are o.k. now, and we all ate the same food and same snacks. To this day, we all reminisce about the good old days. one time, we got over 50 boxes that the whole pallet was refused at the grocery store, we got it for free…yes free…and it was a brand name cereal---fruity pebbles…. I loved it so much that I ate that sugary sweetness at breakfast and afternoon snack, and non- school night, evening snack. I loved eating every last puffed rice piece and it would create a lovely sweet and colorful ending to a love affair…in BOWL LAKE, ARKANSAS.

FROM FATHERS POCKETS

I can remember sneaking into my dad's room while he was on the toilet or eating breakfast and I would take enough change for lunch for my little brother, then older brother, then enough for myself. It was like $2.25 for two lunches. I would just make sure I had two glasses of milk that morning for breakfast so I could make it until snack time after school, before chores and a few hours before dinner time. If my dad did not have any change or cash bills, we would all go hungry…. either that or we would buy a Blue Bell Ice Cream crunchy and chocolatey dip with peanuts covering the sweet and creamy vanilla ice cream. We would never ask my mom, because she was usually getting us ready for school with breakfasts, making sure we had all our school supplies and we looked presentable. Mom made poverty-level income and was raising three boys into men. My dad was a functioning alcoholic and never really did provide for us…well, as far as I can remember. He made less than poverty level because he raised and sold cattle. So those days we only had a quarter, we would make excuses to our friends that we are not hungry, or we had such a big breakfast that we were not hungry. Then we would talk with them for a few minutes, and go grab our cone then eat it slowly and with calmness of enjoying the fact that you at least have this cone to eat when there are hundreds of millions of people going hungry every day….maybe even more than that…I am not sure, but that is a possibility. We all would remind my dad that we needed money or a check for paying for school lunches…. he said he would get it in the morning…. some-times when we would ask him, he would remember, but most of the time we stopped asking. This is the good thing about being an American…you can start working at age 15 and get a license at 15.

So, I got my driver's license and got two jobs, real social security deduction job…my dad still claimed us as dependents…I did not know at the time, but that means he gets to keep our refund…he never had to pay for lunches again…we did that on our own. If and when I have kids, my wife and I will make sure that our kids take their own lunch to school or they get the monies needed for their school lunches…and they better not get that desperate to steal from their Father's Pants!

FRIENDS AND FRIEND'S PARENTS CHANGE DRAWER

I would not care, it was like I was addicted on alcohol or a drug, waiting until my next high and doing illegal things while under the influence…I looked to my friend's and best friends who always had change in their ashtray in their vehicle. I would ride with a few of them a few days of the week before I had my own ride and license. I did that when I was fifteen. I would even steal change from them right after they counted the amount of monies they had in the drawer and I thought I was so smart…I know that they knew that I was stealing their change, but I know deep in their hearts they knew why…cause I was Totino Ramen Poor and they suspected me using it for weekly lunch money.

ASHTRAY IN FRIENDS PARENTS VEHICLE AND HOME

This was probably the least guilty of my stealing…cause it was from parent's…this extra change in their ashtray was probably money they owed to the fast food person as a tip. Or it was just change they collected from early in the day when they went to Starbucks and spent over 5$ on basically a cup of black coffee, it was coffee with whipped cream, who knew! This made me at ease about stealing from my friends parents ashtrays. I only did this a few times, but I still feel guilty about it, although without that stolen money, I don't think I would have ever eaten school lunches in high school. I would also steal from one of my best friends fathers…he would empty his pockets every day and then put it into a pile by the coffee table, on the night stand. He would count it every month and either take his whole family and sometimes myself out to eat at a Mexican restaurant for some good food, or alternatively he would spend the entire amount of money on a fishing or range trip and we would fish all day or go to the range and shoot until we were bored with shooting. I felt a little guilty about stealing from him too, but once again, I think they knew that I stole only because I needed the money for living expenses, not because I was on drugs or drinking or even using tobacco. I stole from everyone that I knew would not miss it…the ones least effected by my criminal act of survival.

ANYONE YOU KNEW VEHICLE

Sometimes during the mornings, everyone would drive once or twice thru the parking lot of all the students. The rich kids, the kids with brand new rides, the kids whose parents or whose grandparents died, and they inherited their old classic car or truck. Or the kid who is a Junior in High School or a Senior and they have been working AG COOP program and have a decent paying job, so they go out on credit and buy a brand-new truck that they financed at 18% for the next 6 years. They my friends are the ones who lose out. I was the most popular kid in school and would ride shotgun or even drive their ride thru the parking lot and while they were not looking, I would take $1.25 in change since this is exactly how much school hot lunch cost at the time. I miss school lunches, all the cafeteria ladies working over hot stoves and ovens so that the communities finest education can be accompanied by the finest eating and culinary experiences. I especially was shocked to see how many kids do not drink their milk during the lunch. They would spend 25 cents on a sweet tea…and drink that instead. So on days where I did not manage to get $1.25 for my school lunch, I would ask people if I could have their milk…I would end up drinking a gallon of milk for lunch…I guess this is why I got ripped and shredded and had a lot more muscle mass than the other kids who were entitled to a free school lunch and they were not drinking their milk. If I remember correctly, you had to have a ticket for your school lunch…with this ticket or cafeteria ticket, you presented it to the first cafeteria lady then you would wait in line until you were served your meal. It was the best, all the cute kids and all the rich family kids would get pretty much seconds with their firsts on desserts and if the meal were like pizza, a larger than average slice. This is how life is too… making the small things the important things, you are eating the bigger pizza…the one who gets pizza bites is the one who worries about the small things and totally ignores the good things which he should be focusing on anyway. I learned this at an early age and have tried to befriend the majority of people that I meet, whether it be at the VA, Brookshire Brothers Grocery Store, Wal-Mart or H.E.B. I will make friends out of strangers in a matter of minutes. I learned to listen to other people and their problems, and even if you don't have an answer now and then, at least you bore the burden with them for that period of healing. I would bring the cafeteria ladies gifts and they probably already knew that this was going to be my largest meal of the day and they would spoon or plate almost 2 complete servings of food for me. I always got 1 chocolate and one 2% milk at the end of the line and sometimes I would grab three…heck if it were not for the milk, I don't think a lot of kids would make it…that is how poor people in our society are. You are blessed to have a job, to have insurance, to be counted on at work for a skill that you bequest and provide.

Be thankful…for the little things, and the big things will follow suit.

I made the most money for an hours work by doing lawns. I once pushed a mower, yes, an old and heavy push-mower with a fuel can almost 1 mile down the road to mow an entire acre of thick grass for a measly $20.00…but if I worked at any other job then that would be 6 hours-worth of work to get that same $20.00. I stuck with mowing so I also could get exercise and build endurance for sports like cross country, track or soccer. Twenty dollars for four hours work was pretty cool for a 13-year-old boy. That was enough fishing gear to last a few months and enough money for pellets for my rifle and lunch money for two weeks…all in a twenty-dollar bill…a Jackson…a real bill that adds value to any salary. I would rake leaves in the winter and fall and would make 5 dollars a small yard, 10 dollars for a medium yard, and yes, you guessed it genius, 15$ for a larger to very large home. Sometimes it would take the whole day, but at 13 that's all you got, time, hormones and energy. Picking dewberries was the best, cause you could be like an Uber eats driver and sample all the goodies while you are in process of picking the fruit. Uberter believe it. My brothers and best friends who were my neighbor, would all pick with me…we almost always got into a dewberry war by throwing the ripest berries at the person we were not getting along with or just the odd man out that no one likes…to be honest with you. We would take the berries to our Marketing Director for process of sale would take place the next work day, and yes, you guessed it, the Marketing Director is mom. She would sell a pint for 2$ and a quart for 5$. In a good day I can pick 20 quarts. Luckily, we live near an old city shooting range and the whole range is overgrown with dewberry bushes…man did we have fun here…we ate sweet berries and talked of future girlfriends and how we all hated the fact that we had 8 more years of education before trade school or college. We had more of this crap and dreaded every minute of it. I never did like school, but I ended up earning 4 science degrees, 2 Masters, one bachelor's and one Associates of Science. I consider myself average.

WASHED AND DETAILED AIRPLANES, PICKED BERRIES AND PICKED PECANS AND ALSO CUT GRASS

Since we lived only a little over one mile from the local airport, I would solicit my service for washing and waxing airplanes for a small fee…yes, small compared to what they would have paid for the same services in a larger more metropolitan area…yes, $150.00-$300.00 per plane…this is very cheap that no one could resist getting a detail job. I swear we did so many planes that we ate pretty darn good that night…meal with appetizer, main course, second course then blue bell ice cream for dessert. My little brother and I would do two to three planes in one weekend if we both hustled and worked hard. We would split the profits down the middle, although I know I did more work than he did…I was just trying to teach him of being a business partner and great little brother helping his big brother. One time I bid 150$ for total polishing of an all-aluminum plane…it was a low wing and when I finished, I was excited and I know I did a really good job because the lady pilot asked me if she should pay me more and I told her my word is my bond…just let me detail your plane next time you get your annual. She said ok and paid me 200$ extra for my little brother so I handed him the money and we went home to get ready to brag to our older brother, mother and father during dinner that we both under age kids made more money than both their parents combined for the entire week worth of work. Picking pecans was the best and most lucrative business…it took about 2 hours to pick a full bucket of paper shell pecans and about 2.5-3 hours to pick a full 5 gallon bucket of the much smaller native pecans…the price was reflective also….25 cents for a pound of paper shells and 28-30 cents per pound for the native pecans….we would make the most of it and bring along our .22 rifles and shoot a few squirrels in the process…that was dinner for five people in just one squirrel…my dad liked them fried with a flour batter and my mom liked the squirrel in a stew and I liked it as squirrels and dumplings…shoot this season I might just get all dressed like Daniel Boone and wear the leather jacket, pants and moccasins with a coon skin or coyote skin hat accompanied by my hunting bag just for black powder and my trusty…22 like .32 caliber Davide Pedersoli percussion black powder rifle, that I bought just for hunting small game but big enough to be used for deer and hogs. I would love to shoot a deer or a hog with the smaller .32 caliber. I would get it on film too…to prove I didn't just shoot it with a high-powered rifle and then shoot the same hole with a black powder rifle. Believe me, I am sure the game warden has fined or jailed many an offender that has tried this one little trick that never works.

HAUL HAY

Hauling square bales of hay was not only profitable at 25 cents a bale and when you haul thousands of bales it adds up pretty quick. One thing that you have to have is strength to pick up 75-80-pound bales and throw and stack them onto the flat-bed trailer. I once hauled 2,000 bales in one day with my friend. We would alternate throwing and driving…we took one hour shifts and worked from sunup till sundown. I think that we were fortunate since it was for my dad and he still paid us. The other good thing about hauling hay is that one the way from the hay field to the barn for storage, we would stop to buy a Gatorade… yes it was in a small glass bottle with a screw on lid…not anymore… full of plastics and chemicals, but still tastes good. We would get a Gatorade…my all-time favorite was melon or fruit punch…I still crave one and it always brings back memories of hauling hay for weeks on end in the summer. One time my friend had a loader that was on the side of the trailer and it would scoop up the square bale and then all we had to do was throw it a shorter distance otherwise onto the trailer…it made it easier but it was not worth it…I think we loaded 50 more bales while using the contraption as opposed to just doing it all manually. I would save the majority of my money from hauling hay and I wish that we still had a working ranch with cattle so I could get ripped in the summer months from hauling hay.

JUST TO HAVE ENOUGH MONEY FOR SCHOOL LUNCHES

I did a lot of foolish things for lunch money and a lot of honorable things to counter balance the negative with a taste of positive. You see, even in your rich and affluent city or town , there are kids that don't know where they will get money to pay for their school lunches… some will steal, some will own it and get free lunches on the free lunch program and some will just flat out go hungry until they get home to eat whatever meal their mom or dad can procure…most of the time just enough to keep their stomachs full until the next meal. This is a tragedy of sorts of the population that does not have enough and is too darn proud to tell anyone in order to rectify the situation. One day I will solve that and no one in the United States or the World for that matter will ever go hungry again.

Loonie Farm Adventures

Saturday, June 29, 2019

This short story depicts the struggles of identity and mental health awareness and physical health awareness in animals that is directly related to mental and physical illness/diseases in humans. There is a Cottontail Rabbit who suffers from Bipolar I Disorder with Chronic

Depression and SAD-Seasonal Affective Disorder. There is a Skunk who suffers from Kleptomania and Schizoaffective Disorder Bipolar Type. An armadillo that suffers from Diabetes Type II and Chronic Obesity. There is a squirrel that suffers from hallucinations of perilous acts and discrimination from society. There is an old Labrador Retriever that loves every animal and he suffers from Anxiety with Panic Attacks and Classic Narcissism.

Chapter One: A Country Life.

The coming home of Ranger, the Labrador Retriever that at age 2 suffered from Anxiety so bad that his Veterinarian had to send him to an Animal Behavior Specialist, one of only three in the entire State of Texas. Ranger also suffered from Panic Attacks and Classic Narcisse. He was trained since six weeks of age to retrieve anything that was not as heavy as he and would potentially either float or bounce. I trained Ranger every day after Grad School to fetch.... starting off with a small tennis ball and just throwing it a few feet and letting him get praised or rewarded for accomplishing fetching with ease. I promoted him to a Red-Head bumper and threw that into a small pond and he swam to retrieve the bumper. I progressively made it more and more difficult and added a .22 rifle to the mix and would throw the bumper...shoot a round into the water and have him fetch it. I did this same routine of throwing the bumper than shooting and having Ranger retrieve without fail. I moved up to a .410 shotgun and did so for a week or so then moved up to a .20 gauge for a week then a .12 gauge for two weeks. I would play fetch of sometimes and I also transitioned to sitting on a bucket, used for dove hunting since you store your ammo and drinks and dead birds into while you hunt. I shot off of this bucket with the 12 gauge and he retrieved the bumper every shot. In a few long weeks, dove season would open and I know we were ready. Ranger must have known that something was up, since I got up before the sun rose and had a shotgun, a bucket and a huge glass of hot Nescafe Instant Coffee in a cup with cream and a little honey. I shot the first dove and Ranger Retrieved it flawlessly. It was his first hunt and he was a master already. The next two dove were a double and he was on point the whole time...he marked one bird and searched for the other one then retrieved both with no concern. I shot a few more singles and he fetched all of them. I then shot and wounded a bird that would have been my limit for the day and the dove landed in the bottom section of a live oak on the neighbor's property. Ranger never quit and barked under that tree...for a few minutes until I got over there to investigate. I saw the dove and had a handy pellet pistol for situations like this and I shot the dove and he fetched it and brought it to me. Needless to say, we ate good that night. I did my casual grilling of dove breast, wrapped in jalapeno and bacon and filled with cream cheese and put on the grill for about 10 minutes indirect heat. I now have a contraption which was a gift for Christmas a few years earlier from my eldest niece. It is a pepper roaster and has 20 compartments to put your stuffed and wrapped jalapeno-popper-peppers. Ranger unfortunately was with a bad influence of a dog that I had bought at the Dog Farm in the Local Mall......his name was Hunter and he was a beautiful German Shorthaired pointer. I was working 2 jobs so when he was a puppy, he did not get the attention needed to properly train a bird dog. He was pretty much wild and ran all over the place and never stopped. He and Ranger went to the neighbors and since they were young, they chased the neighbors' chickens and tried to kill one of them. The neighbor shot them both with a .22 rifle and wounded them to where they were never going to think about chasing chickens. Hunter ran into town a few weeks later and I was called since he had my number on his identification collar. He was 20 miles from home. I had to get rid of him since he was a liability and could cause someone to have an accident and potentially hurt or kill someone.

Ever since the day Ranger got shot for chasing chickens at the neighbors, he is scared of guns and thunder. He is a great companion dog but worthless for a hunting and retrieving dog. Either way, we all love him and adore him and spoil him all the time. He is a sweetheart of a pet and was actually considered for being my service dog and therapy dog. He is so sweet that one time when I was mowing the acreage of our farm with the riding mower and I saw him at a distance picking up something brown and moving it to where I had already cut the grass…..as I got closer to the spot and closer, I could see that he was grabbing all the baby cottontail bunny rabbits out of their nest site and preventing them from being run over and cut to pieces by the mower. This is how loving and compassionate dogs are and especially of the Labrador Retriever Breed. He did this and I had to give him a treat, so I thawed out some dry deer sausage and cut it up into bite sized pieces and I played fetch with Ranger and every time he retrieved, I would give him a one-inch slice of deer dry sausage. He ate the whole link and still wanted to play fetch until it got too dark to really see anymore.

There is a Cottontail Rabbit who suffers from Bipolar I Disorder with Chronic Depression and SAD-Seasonal Affective Disorder.

The fluffy little cottontail rabbit that often frequents the garden to eat all the greens and as many green tomatoes as possible. He frequently talks to himself, is melancholic about everything, even the really important things and abuses drugs and alcohol to "cope" with "dope". He often does not shower for days at a time and brushes his teeth only at night, and never in the morning…I guess this could be the clue to him only having 12 normal teeth and suffering from tooth decay and gum loss…. tooth decay and gum loss that was totally preventable if he were not so damn lazy. He is funny to himself only, he laughs a lot but at his own jokes and he is not funny at all even though he thinks he is. This really gets old after a while….but who cares anyway, cause the Rabbit will forget about it and get all pissed off at you and yell at you for no good particular reason other than yes, this is a flare up of one of the poles….now we have to deal with mood swings and paranoia. Then after bouts of these symptoms, more chronic depression which can be exonerated from anywhere that you want to have normal people…. without Depression

THE DEER IN THE WOODS AND THE FISH IN THE POND

as a yearly guest, Bipolar one disorder with melancholic features would not exist. The rabbit has it all and knows how to beat the system...what system...your system....my system...just some more rambling on and on about firecrackers. Not making a lick of sense...I am not sure what the tongue looks like, but a lick of sense could destroy a whole fudgesicle. And you cannot forget about the seasonal affective disorder... where you get sick certain times of the year...for me in winter time and early fall, late summer I suffer the most compared to the rest of the year where I have been sick during off months, but not the majority of times. I have been hospitalized over 15 times and stayed as long as 45 days at the VA and over 3 months straight at Walter Reed Army Medical Center in Maryland. I loved it there...baked salmon on Fridays...Monday thru Friday all you can eat bacon, and real maple oak smoked thick ass bacon, you know the bacon that all the rich folks eat...yeah, it was that good... and the butteriest of biscuits with honey or jam. And you know they had the best coffee around....and I sure did drink my fair share of it while I was there. I made the mistake of cutting off my in-patient medical tag I.D. and this is when I started having to pay at the dining hall in the hospital cafeteria. I remember all you could drink chocolate milk too....and yes, I would fill up my camelback too...it's a water container that you can drink from while doing almost any activity, all hands-free and with little difficulty. This is the cheapskate that I used to be...I lost this once I got my 100% checks from the VA. Easy come. Easy go...I even buy several hundred-dollar knives to send to friends that I haven't talked to in a while. Or custom camo seat covers for my cousins Toyota tundra since he is a hunter and fisherman like me...we got to stick together....I really should be saving for a cabin or beach house...but I live each day as if it is my last and this seems to be quite expensive and I am always broke at the end of the month although I bring home almost $3,000.00. I figured that I have received close to $500,000.00 dollars and only have very little to show for it...but hey that's how the cookie crumbles when you are as generous and honest as I am. I used to loan money that I had so much... then even $10,000.00 was chump change and I always had twenty or thirty thousand in the bank slush fund.

A LABRADOR RETREIVER WITH NARCICISM

Ranger is now middle aged for his breed and he loves to bark at any power tool like a weed-eater, mower, saw, edger or trimmer. He will follow whoever is using the equipment and bark and bark and then when he is exhausted and hot, he will go to the pond nearby and take a swim and get a drink or two. He will then continue to bark if there is any noise like that. He will guard all the animals and stay awake at night to protect our farm and all that it means to him and to us…it is our livelihood and our welfare depends on it.

It is my incumbent responsibility to take care of the landscaping and gardening. This is pretty much a two to three day a week job if done to standard and done well. So, you guessed it…our yard looks amazing and is manicured in every way. Ranger helps me do the whole thing. He has almost been hit by traffic going down the road and not really paying any attention. This is why I always look behind me and in front of me when I am mowing close to the road. We have had some near misses when Ranger will see a dragonfly, butterfly or grasshopper and he will chase it, even jumping four to five feet off the ground in an aerobatic way of catching a bug. He did this once and jumped right in the middle of the road and almost got hit. Now I have a way of preventing this…. I just wear him out and let him go to the pond then I mow near the road. He will be swimming and I will be trimming.

Ranger suffers from panic attacks and anxiety when it is thundering outside. You see, with gunshots, especially during dove season, he will get these, but he recovers very fast since he can lay on the tile floor of the laundry room for as long as he wants to. He really didn't show signs of anxiety or panic attacks until weeks after he was shot by the neighbor for chasing chickens. I never noticed it until he was barking loudly during a thunderstorm. He immediately came inside the house when I opened the door. He was shaking and was very scared since he had his tail between his legs, and I know this as a sign of fear. I got out a sleeping bag and laid it by the dryer and he kept me company as I washed, dried and folded clothes for a bit while the storm thundered its hear out. It was a light storm but taught me a valuable lesson that even the littlest of scary things can be mightier than the persons level of patience dealing with the fear and can lead to PTSD or Anxiety and Panic Attacks. As for the Narcissism tendencies.... he is a Labrador and if it isn't about Ranger or something important to him, then it doesn't exist. First thing in the morning, I pet him, all day I pet him, at night I play fetch with him and feed and pet him. Actually, feeding is simple since we live on a farm, he just eats when and how ever much he wants to. In Veterinary Medicine this is called "free-feeding". I prefer this method since the dog is always full or not hungry. This is hard to tell when you feed your animal two times a day, breakfast and dinner. Most of the time they scarf it all down in a few bites. With Ranger, he nibbles for a bit, then plays or rests then nibbles then, some more, and so on. He is his own dietary master of sorts and manages to do pretty well doing things this way since he got perfect health on his last DVM checkup. I did get him some heart-guard heartworm preventative and some flea and tick tablets that supposedly last 3 months before having to administer another tablet. If he can make it until September, then the fleas are not that bad then and the ticks are all eaten by our yard birds/chickens and guinea fowl who patrol the entire farm looking for small bugs and insects/arthropods to gobble up and enjoy. Ranger is my best friend and he is always in a great mood, playful and energetic...and he loves to play fetch every day, no matter what, he always plays fetch with me. It is refreshing to know that he taught me to always be in a good mood no matter what the circumstances and eventually you will always be in a good mood.

There is a Skunk who suffers from Kleptomania and Schizoaffective Disorder Bipolar Type.

Kleptomania is a condition where a subject steals for no good reason or for a specific reason...most of the time for just the thrill of the act of stealing itself...Everyone...Yes...Everyone has stolen something at least once in their life and some people still steal to this day, even in adult hood and late adult hood. The skunk named Sammy is kleptomaniac to the max and steals stuff on a regular basis...just the other day he stole food from the chickens feed container, and they all starved for the day just so he would keep a full belly. The day before that he stole some insulation out of the barn to use in his den/nest. He also suffers from Schizoaffective disorder, Bipolar type. I am not sure exactly how this is any different than regular Bipolar, but I will try to explain it to you in laymen's terms when they suffer from hallucinations or delusions and symptoms of either mania or depression. So, it is not that different than regular Bipolar disorder except for the delusions and hallucinations. He would often see other animals in the dark that we all know as predators, dogs, coyotes, wolves, timber wolves, hawks, owls, humans and anything else that would pose an immediate threat to a skunks life. He saw them on a regular basis and is coping with it by keeping himself in the here and now and concentrating on something positive and joyous.

An armadillo that suffers from Diabetes Type II and Chronic Obesity.

There is a northern naked-tailed armadillo and the nine-banded armadillo whose range is almost in every central and Eastern- Central and coastal states in the U.S. especially in the South-Central States... most notably Texas. The most widespread is the nine banded armadillo which is found not only in North America, but also South America and Central America, making it the most thriving of its kind. Just like many thriving species, there are diseases that affect them all for population control purposes such as is the case with Amy the Armadillo with Diabetes. She was genetically pre-dispositioned to have diabetes. She ate all organic and lots of fruits and veggies and has diabetes so bad that her blood sugar is elevated even after taking insulin injections. You see, Amy is like the other 30% of the population suffering from diabetes and associated diseases like nerve pain and heart disease and obesity. She weighs almost twice as much as another armadillo her age and species and can barely move around without any difficulty. There is not a cure for diabetes, but Amy the Armadillo is conducting medical research and is on her way to curing this disease and preventing it from happening in the first place.

There is a squirrel that suffers from hallucinations of perilous acts and discrimination from society

The main thing the paranoid squirrel has been affected by is discrimination from society, mainly because she is gray, old and thinks that death is knocking on the front door of her existence. She is beautiful, single mom, who is Hispanic. She is 57 years old and still works and is in love with a younger Fox Squirrel. I think they are going to get married….it is a true love story. They met in the woods in Mexico on vacation and danced a few times and it was instant love…the problem is that her younger lover loves a different Squirrel named Gema….his true love of a lifetime…she is a school teacher and can possible have one baby since she is of the age where it is risky to give birth….she will reunite with her true love soon and they will live a happy life of love, peace, prosperity, wealth, religion, family and GOD. Any illness is over come with LOVE…that is the cure to mental illness….all these diagnoses and parties described in this short story are ficticious and just a reminder that EVERYONE has some kind of mental illness….. EVERYONE…so remember that and your heart and mind will open and you will see the world that we live in…we are all individuals and we all need to HONOR thy NEIGHBOR…this means honor the good in everyone and not be a fly drawn to trash and be the HONEYBEE drawn to love and nectar and flies over the garbage in life….ignoring it….making honey---happiness from always looking at the positive in life…their life and others lives.

31 Days to a Womans Heart

By: Uncle TOTINO RAMEN

Week 1

Day 1
Cook pancakes with maple syrup, scrambled eggs and sausage or bacon for breakfast in bed.

Day 2
Write a poem and place it with tape onto your partners mirror in the bathroom when she does her make-up in the morning.

Day 3
Pack a lunch made fresh with a garden salad with grilled chicken breast or even just a simple sandwich with a bag of chips with a drink or accompanied by a note saying that you cannot live without your partner. If you cannot make a gourmet sandwich, just make a Peanut Butter and Jelly with a bag of Frito chips.

Day 4
Take some rose petals and lay them from the living room to the bathroom with a warm bubble bath ready for your loved one.

Day 5
Go on an evening after work walk and hold hands.

Day 6
Call your partner rather than texting her during her break and tell her you cannot live without her.

Day 7
Get your partner a card and write her a note saying that she is the love of your life and you are very lucky to have her in your life.

Week 2

Day 8
Call your partner at work and tell her that you love her. When you get home do all the laundry, cook a simple dinner and have a flower, bottle of wine and a candle on the table, ready for a romance. You could make something as simple as canned soup with crackers and a Caesar-salad or cook a more advanced meal. Whatever you do, be romantic and take every step to make it special.

Day 9
Wake up and cook scrambled eggs, with buttered toast and jam and sit down and eat breakfast with your partner. Tell her to have a blessed day filled with happiness and peace.

Day 10
Before your partner gets home, get some body lotion and a warm towel from the dryer and leave a note on the front door, saying, welcome home to a 30-minute full-body massage. Pamper your partner and give her a light massage with a gentle touch of love.

Day 11
When your partner gets up, tell her she is the most beautiful woman on earth and kiss her, telling her that you cannot live without her. If she takes a shower or bath first thing in the morning, take it with her and wash her body or her hair, if she needs it to be washed. Resume the romance by drying her off after the bath/shower.

Day 12
If you are good at poetry, write a poem, a simple poem and place it in your wife's wallet or purse or work bag or gym bag. It will be a surprise and make her day that much more special, even if she has a stressful day.

Day 13
Take the night off from cooking and make sure that you get dressed up in business casual and make a date night of going to dinner. Bring a flower and a note and give it to your waiter/waitress and have them bring it to your partner at the end of the meal. The best way to do this is to have the note and flower in your truck/car and excuse yourself to go to the bathroom and give them to the waiter/waitress at that time.

Day 14
If you have the money, have a bouquet of her favorite flowers sent to your partner at work. If not, and you work nearby, take her to lunch…

if all this is not possible, program her phone to play her favorite song. She will be surprised that you are paying attention to detail. Just put a note in her wallet or purse or on the back of her phone advising her to play the song as a testament of your love for her.

Week 3

Day 15
Get up early. If you both drink coffee, or tea, make some coffee and or tea and sit quietly on the porch or in the kitchen and make plans for a romantic getaway. It could be as simple as watching a movie or favorite show or even just taking a bath together and relaxing in the tub for half an hour.

Day 16
Before your partner gets home, bake some cookies or sweet rolls, even from a can or better yet, homemade and surprise her with the baked goods after a delicious dinner of your liking.

Day 17
Take your partner to a home improvement store or plant vendor and pick out a flower or plant to bring home to plant in regard to your undying love for one another. If you live in a small place, a potted plant will do. If you are blessed to have a home or green space, plant a fruit tree or other ornamental and dedicate it to your love and affection towards your partner.

Day 18
Get a board game and play a game after a simple dinner of soup and grilled cheese sandwiches. This will allow for less time cleaning up and more time to spend together before bed.

Day 19
If your partner wears perfume, get some good smelling perfume and wrap it in gift wrap and present it during dinner. You are good at cooking by

now and can make a pasta dish with whatever you want to put in it like hamburger meat or grilled chicken, with the beef a red tomato sauce, with chicken, alfredo sauce. You should pair the meal with a red wine and a garden salad. After dinner, present the perfume with a note that says she is as wonderful to the eyes as the perfume is to the sense of smell.

Day 20
Get up before your partner and make a fruit and vegetable smoothie before the day begins. Garnish the drink with a sprig of mint leaves. Accompany the fruit and veggie smoothie with a hand-written note saying your partner is as delicious and healthy to the body as nourishing as the drink.

Day 21
Shop online or preferable with your partner for sexy lingerie at a reputable store and watch in amazement of how happy your partner will be that you care about them looking sexy for you during intimacy.

Week 4

Day 22
Call your partner and just say that you were thinking of them and one thing that they do to turn you on and hope that the rest of their day is as special and blessed as they have made you feel with the warmth of their love.

Day 23
Send an email to your partner just saying that you love them and cannot wait to kiss them when they get home for the day. Surprise them with their favorite dessert that you will make while they are unwinding for the day after work. It could be as simple as cinnamon rolls from a can, to a cobbler baked from scratch with a scoop of ice cream or topped with whipped cream.

Day 24
When you go to bed together, just sleep naked and do not make love, just touch each other and praise your partner of how sexy they look, and they will feel sexier and remember to not take it past touching. This will show your partner that they are more than just a sex object and it will make them feel more appreciated.

Day 25
Take an envelope and write a letter of the top 10 things you love about your partner…mail it to their place of work or at home and let them indulge in feeling special.

Day 26
Buy some helium balloons and bring them home….leave them in your truck/car and wait until your partner goes to bed….tell them that you love them. Leave the balloons in the kitchen, tied to the coffee maker or fridge with a note telling them that you are celebrating your undying love for your partner.

Day 27
Plan a picnic in the back yard or go all out and drive to a remote area or even a park. Pack fine cheeses, meats, crackers, mustards, some wine or non-alcoholic grape juice and bring a blanket, pillows and just relax for an hour or two before going home for the day.

Day 28
Even if you have things around the house today, just tell your partner that you will do it for them the next day and take the rest of the day off to just forget about all the stress. Go to the movies and go out to eat. Make it more like a date, reminding your partner that life is precious, more precious with them in it and just relax at the movies. Remember to hold hands and be loving.

Day 29

Play a romantic or favorite song to your partner and sing it to them, even if you cannot sing that well. It will show that you are thinking outside the box and showing that you are willing to go out on a limb to be romantic and affectionate.

Day 30

Pick or buy a few flowers and place them on your lovers pillow before bed and write a thing you love about them on a sticky note and place one on each flower....three flowers should do the trick.

Day 31

Tell your partner how sexy they are and that you cannot wait to make love to them either at home or on a weekend getaway. You need to take your time and undress them slowly and gently and touch every part of their body with hands of gentleness. Give them your undivided attention and take your time as if it were the first time and watch them fill with happiness and joy being expressed right before your eyes.

I Prefer to Pee Outside

BY: TOTINO RAMEN

THIS IS A SHORT LIST THAT DETERMINES IF YOU'RE A COUNTRY FOLK OR CITY FOLK

1. IF YOU PREFER YOUR GREASE TO BE MADE INTO GRAVY… NOT BIOFUELS OR ALTERNATIVE ENERGY SOURCES.
2. IF YOU PREFER TO GET YOUR BUZZ ON WHISKEY OR BEER OR A WHILE FISHING FOR LARGEMOUTH BASS….. NOT WINE AND MIXED DRINKS.

3. IF YOUR SOCIAL HOUR CONSISTS OF FISHING OR HUNTING OR TARGET PRACTICE INSTEAD OF A WALK IN THE PARK OR VISIT TO THE MOVIES.
4. IF YOUR IDEA OF GRABBING A BITE TO EAT IS TACO BELL INSTEAD OF GRILLING A STEAK OR BURGERS AND HOT DOGS……
5. IF YOUR IDEA OF RELAXATION IS NOT SITTING IN BACK TO BACK TRAFFIC AND INSTEAD SITTING ON THE FRONT OR BACK PORCH WATCHING THE SUNRISE/SET AND CHILLING WITH A COLD ONE IN YOUR HAND….. NOT A COLD ONE IN YOUR NEIGHBORS HOUSE…I.E. CORPSE…WHICH WOULD BE INDICATIVE OF HIGH CRIME RATES AND VIOLENCE.
6. IF YOUR IDEA OF A SKINNY IS NOT A LATTE FROM STARBUICKS AND INSTEAD IS A FISH THAT IS NOT GROWING ACCORDINGLY OR A DEER, RABBIT, SQUIRRELL OR ANY OTHER GAME THAT YOU ARE HAVING FOR SUPPER THAT YOU JUST SHOT IN THE BACK 40 IS SKINNIER THAN A FATTER VERSION OF ITSELF.
7. IF YOUR IDEA OF FUN IN THE SUN IS TAKING YOUR SHIRT OFF AT THE LAKE OR PRIVATE POND AND GETTING A FEW HOOKS WET…..IF NOT IT PROBABLY MEANS A CRUISE TO COZUMEL FROM GALVESTON, TEXAS AND ENJOYING BEING A LAZY GLUTTON FOR A FEW DAYS.
8. IF YOU CALL SHOTGUN….A CITY FOLK WILL THINK YOU ARE ASKING FOR THE FRONT PASSENGER SEAT…… BUT IF YOU ARE COUNTRY….THEN YOU ARE ASKING FOR WHICH ONE??? 10, 12, 16, 28, 20 OR .410?????THEN IF YOU ARE REALLY COUNTRY WITH SOME MONEY…YOU WILL THEN SAY WHICH ONE??? BENELLI, HARRINGTON AND RICHARDSON, REMINGTON OR MOSSBURG????? AND IF YOU ARE SOO COUNTRY THAT YOU CAN'T

SPELL YOUR FIRST NAME....BUT CAN SHOOT AT A MOVING COON FROM DAMN NEAR A MILE DOWN THE ROAD.......AND KILL IT....WITH ONE SHOT.....AND DRINK A BEER.....YES LIKE DOS XX OR MILWAULKEES BEAST....I MEAN BEST???? OR WUZ IT THE WORST? REAL MEXICAN----BEER....LIKE DOS XX VERSUS THE OPPOSITE END OF THE BEER SPECTRUM.....MILWUALKEES BEST....THE BEAST......THE CHEAP STUFF THAT EVEN HIGH SCHOOL FRESHMAN WOULD PASS ON AND WOULD RATHER DRINK GOAT PISS FROM A WARM CUP.....

9. WHEN TAKING A DIP TO A CITY PERSON MEANS SWIMMING IN THE POOL....US REDNECKS ARE SO SOPHISTICATED THAT WE HAVE A FEW USES FOR THE WORD DIP. HAVE A DIP OF THIS QUESO.....TAKE A DIP INTO THE POOL, TAKE A DIP INTO THE POND, TAKE A DIP INTO THE LAKE, TAKE A DIP INTO THE OCEAN/SEA/GULF. OR WHEN I DIP YOU DIP, WE DIP....WHEN YOU DIP YOU MIGHT BE DIPPING TOBACCO LIKE COPENHAGEN OR SKOAL.

10. BOOTING UP---IF YOU ARE FROM THE CITY THIS MEANS THAT YOU ARE STARTING YOUR COMPUTER....IF YOU ARE COUNTRY THIS MEANS THAT YOU ARE PUTTING ON YOUR COWBOY BOOTS.

11. I HAVE UNLIMITED GIGS----WHEN YOU ARE FROM THE CITY THIS MEANS THAT YOU HAVE A LOT OF POWER ON YOUR CELL PHONE....IF YOU ARE FROM THE COUNTRY THIS MEANS THAT YOU CAN GIG FROGS FOR THE WHOLE NIGHT...OR YOU PULL OUT YOUR GUITAR AND DO A BLAKE SHELTON OR GEORGE STRAIT SONG AT WITH YOUR BAND...THIS FOR A COUNTRY BOY IS A MUSICAL GIG...OR YLU WNT TO TEXAS A&M AND YOU GIG'EM TO OTHER AGGIES....ITS AN AGGIE THING...YOUR WOULDN'T UNDERSTAND... TRUST ME....

12. FISHING/PFISHING---WHEN YOU SAY, YES, YOU ARE USING A ROD, A NET, POLE, ARROW, SPEAR OR BY HAND (NOODLING)---YOU ARE ACTUALLY FISHING.... WHEN YOU ARE FROM THE CITY AND FISHING IN THE WAY OF PFISHING FOR SENSITIVE INFORMATION ON THE DARK WEB....THAT'S WHAT I THINK AND THAT'S HOW I FEEL.!!!!!!!!!

Yummy Yummy Says My Tummy

INSPIRED BY MY NIECES AND NEPHEWS

LOVE: TOTINO RAMEN/UNCLE BEAU

SIMPLE KIDS MEAL AND IDEAS:
FOR BEGINNER CHEFS

DAY ONE

BREAKFAST MENU: Two scrambled eggs with salt and pepper and piece of toast with butter and a glass of orange juice or milk.

LUNCH MENU: One peanut butter and jelly sandwich with a glass of milk and nonother than Fritos Corn Chips.

AFTERNOON SNACK MENU: Bowl of cereal like fruit loops, frosted flakes, honey nut cheerios or raisin bran.

DINNER MENU: Garden salad with light dressing, Italian, or vinaigrette dressing. A bowl of vegetable soup and a nice grilled piece of fish like salmon or lake trout.

DAY TWO

BREAKFAST MENU: Two hard-boiled eggs with bacon/turkey preferably and toast with glass of milk.

LUNCH MENU: Pot Roast with Vegetables and a glass of water.

AFTERNOON SNACK MENU: One cheese snack stick with an apple and peanut butter.

DINNER MENU: One serving of hamburger meat with sauce spaghetti with a serving of parmesan cheese and garlic toast with a glass of water.

DAY THREE

BREAKFAST MENU: Two poached eggs with buttered toast and jam with a glass of orange juice or milk.

LUNCH MENU: One turkey and dressing with sweet potatoes and cream gravy with glass of milk.

AFTERNOON SNACK MENU: One large banana with glass of milk.

DINNER MENU: Burgers with cheese and all the trimmings you want on sesame seed buns with mustard, ketchup, or mayonnaise with some carrot sticks and celery sticks with light ranch dressing as a dip.

DAY FOUR

BREAKFAST MENU: Two egg omelet with peppers and cheese with a piece of butter toast.

LUNCH MENU: Beef tacos with lettuce, tomato, onion and cheese with a glass of milk.

AFTERNOON SNACK MENU: Vegetable chips with a glass of water.

DINNER MENU: Chicken enchiladas with garden fresh salad with glass of milk.

DAY FIVE

BREAKFAST MENU: Buttermilk pancakes with syrup and a serving of scrambled eggs with a glass of orange juice or milk.

LUNCH MENU: Homemade Cheese Pizza with parmesan cheese and a garden salad with Italian dressing.

AFTERNOON SNACK MENU: One apple with a serving of pineapple juice.

DINNER MENU: Beef Lasagna and parmesan cheese with garlic French toast with salad and Italian dressing.

DAY SIX

BREAKFAST MENU: Egg, Cheese. And ground beef tacos with glass of orange juice or milk.

LUNCH MENU: Chicken Spaghetti with toasted bread and Cole slaw salad.

AFTERNOON SNACK MENU: Fresh fruit cup and glass of milk.

DINNER MENU: Fried catfish with tater tots and Greek salad and glass of water.

DAY SEVEN

BREAKFAST MENU: Cheese and egg quesadillas with peppers and a glass of orange juice or milk.

LUNCH MENU: Frito Pie with Frito chips, cheese, chili and jalapenos with a side salad and glass of sweet tea.

AFTERNOON SNACK MENU: Serving of Jell-O of any flavor and a glass of milk.

DINNER MENU: Baked potato with cheese, sour cream, chives, chopped peppers and hamburger meat with a glass of water or milk.

DAY EIGHT

BREAKFAST MENU: Oatmeal and glass of milk.

LUNCH MENU: Soft tacos with lettuce, tomato, cheese and sour cream with a side of refried beans and glass of milk.

AFTERNOON SNACK MENU: Nutella and Peanut butter on graham crackers with a glass of milk.

DINNER MENU: Beef stew with cornbread and glass of milk or water.

DAY NINE

BREAKFAST MENU: Fruit and Veggie smoothie with 2% milk and protein powder.

LUNCH MENU: Beef tips with gravy and rice with grilled vegetables and a glass of milk.

AFTERNOON SNACK MENU: Milk and an oatmeal raisin butter cookie.

DINNER MENU: Grilled chicken breast and garden salad with steamed rice and grilled vegetables and a large glass of water.

DAY TEN

BREAKFAST MENU: Breakfast soft tacos with refried beans, cheese, hamburger and peppers with scrambled eggs.

LUNCH MENU: Chicken Noodle Soup with crackers and glass of milk.

AFTERNOON SNACK MENU: Fried plantain bananas with a glass of milk.

DINNER MENU: Meat Loaf with mashed potatoes and cream gravy with baked vegetables with a glass of milk.

DAY ELEVEN

BREAKFAST MENU: Scrambled eggs, turkey bacon with toast and a glass of milk.

LUNCH MENU: Grilled chicken breast garden salad with glass of sweat tea or milk.

AFTERNOON SNACK MENU: One Oatmeal cookie by Little Debbie snacks and a glass of milk.

DINNER MENU: Penne Pasta with alfredo sauce with grilled chicken breast and garlic bread with garden salad and a glass of water.

DAY TWELVE

BREAKFAST MENU: Breakfast cereal of choice with milk and a small banana.

LUNCH MENU: Fried Chicken with mixed vegetables and French fries with a glass of sweat tea.

AFTERNOON SNACK MENU: Serving of Cheese Nips with sliced sharp cheddar cheese and mustard.

DINNER MENU: Baked salmon with steamed asparagus and sautéed red potatoes and serving of steamed rice with glass of water or milk.

DAY THIRTEEN

BREAKFAST MENU: Hot Grits with butter and a little sugar, with a banana and a glass of milk

LUNCH MENU: Beef Lasagna with garden salad and pineapple upside down cake and a glass of milk.

AFTERNOON SNACK MENU: Saltine crackers with cheddar cheese and mustard.

DINNER MENU: Grilled beef sausage with mashed potatoes and grilled corn on the cobb and steamed mustard greens.

DAY FOURTEEN

BREAKFAST MENU: One Orange, one half banana, one bran muffin with butter and a glass of milk.

LUNCH MENU: Grilled cheese sandwich with chips and a glass of milk with an apple on the side.

AFTERNOON SNACK MENU: Peanut Butter crackers and a glass of milk.

DINNER MENU: Fried Eggs, toast, bacon, sliced cheese and milk with some sliced salt and pepper garden tomatoes.

DAY FIFTEEN

BREAKFAST MENU: Granola bar and a glass of milk, sometimes with spreadable peanut butter and/or with Nutella...make that two granola bars!

LUNCH MENU: Beef Stew with saltines, cornbread, green beans and a peanut butter crunch bar as dessert.

AFTERNOON SNACK MENU: Popcorn with loads of butter and a little salty, but not too much. And you can splurge and get a diet Coke or Diet Dr. Pepper if you are from Texas.

DINNER MENU: Stir Fried beef with onion, peppers, both spicy and mild and garlic and chives with water chestnuts and sugar snap peas in the hull for the main meal along with fried rice or white rice with a ton of water to wash it down with.

DAY SIXTEEN

BREAKFAST MENU: Peanut butter on toasted bread drizzled with fresh honey.

LUNCH MENU: Corn dogs, made of beef or chicken and beef with mustard, ketchup or even mayonnaise with a glass of tea, apple crisp as dessert, a bag of chips and a glass of milk to wash it down with.

AFTERNOON SNACK MENU: Handful of nuts like peanuts with little to no salt. A huge glass of milk to wash it down with, or a large glass of water.

DINNER MENU:

DAY SEVENTEEN

BREAKFAST MENU: Little sizzler sausages, with toast, scrambled or fried egg with salt and pepper with a large glass of fruit juice or milk.

LUNCH MENU: Dirty Rice with sausage as the protein with red beans and rice with canned sweet corn.

AFTERNOON SNACK MENU: Beef jerky with a serving of milk.

DINNER MENU: Baked Chicken with spices like rosemary and other seasonings with corn bread stuffing, sweet potato pie with green bean casserole and a glass of grape juice or milk.

DAY EIGHTEEN

BREAKFAST MENU: Breakfast quesadillas filled with cheese, onion, bell pepper and jalapeno pepper with ground beef or deer or shredded chicken, served with Picante Sauce and sour cream. Also served with a glass of grape, orange, or pineapple juice or alternatively a glass of milk.

LUNCH MENU: Ramen noodle soup with kimchi cabbage and some rice and stir fried beef.

AFTERNOON SNACK MENU: A handful of Green Olives with a serving of hummus and pita chips, preferable pepper hummus with jalapenos and sea salt pita chips.

DINNER MENU: Roasted Lamb chops with mustard greens, mashed potatoes and gravy with glass of grape juice or glass of milk.

DAY NINETEEN

BREAKFAST MENU:

LUNCH MENU: BBQ Beef Brisket sandwich with onions, pickles, extra bbq sauce and a bag of Lays Potato Chips or side of potato salad or cole slaw with dessert being peach or blackberry cobbler with a glass of sweat tea.

AFTERNOON SNACK MENU: Pretzels dipped in peanut butter with a glass of milk to wash it down with.

DINNER MENU: Veal Cutlets with marinara sauce on a bed of spaghetti pasta noodles with a Greek salad and French bread with a glass of grape juice or a glass or milk or even water.

DAY TWENTY

BREAKFAST MENU: Buttered waffles and fried chicken and maple or pancake syrup with a glass of orange juice of milk.

LUNCH MENU: Sliced homemade deer pastrami with left sauerkraut and hoagie roll with a glass of juice or iced tea.

AFTERNOON SNACK MENU: Ramen noodle soup Doctored up with sliced cheese and topped with cooked deer meat and onions with chives and a glass of water.

DINNER MENU:

DAY TWENTY-ONE

BREAKFAST MENU: Buttered biscuits. With a choice of cream gravy or homemade jam or with local honey. Washed down with a cold glass of milk or orange juice.

LUNCH MENU: Deer tips, like beef tips and brown gravy with steamed broccoli and carrots with French bread to eat and dip into the brown gravy bath and white rice on the side also.

AFTERNOON SNACK MENU: One orange and a small ripened banana and a glass of milk.

DINNER MENU: Deer stir-fry and with all the normal vegetables like carrots, broccoli, snap peas in the hull, onions, bell peppers and garlic with leftover rice from lunch and a talk glass of water or even a glass of red-wine.

DAY TWENTY-TWO

BREAKFAST MENU: Buttered pancakes or crepes with fresh cut fruit and real maple syrup or cane and maple syrup mix from Cracker Barrel. Washed down with a cold glass of orange juice or milk.

LUNCH MENU: Grilled cheese sandwich with salsa between the melted cheese and buttery-toasted bread and a glass of milk.

AFTERNOON SNACK MENU: One serving of saltine crackers or wheat thins and sliced parmesan cheese and dry deer sausage with yellow or Dijon mustard.

DINNER MENU: Grilled deer steaks with grilled butter dripping vegetables of your choice and white rice or macaroni and cheese with a glass of red-wine or real grape juice if you cannot drink.

DAY TWENTY-THREE

BREAKFAST MENU: Bowl of quick oats and milk with a dash of cinnamon and a sprinkle of sugar with nuts like almonds, pecans or walnuts.

LUNCH MENU: Turkey and swiss cheese on whole wheat bread with light mayonnaise and mustard with lettuce and tomato with a serving of low-fat chips or alternatively carrot wedges and celery wedges with light ranch dressing.

AFTERNOON SNACK MENU: An apple and a glass of milk.

DINNER MENU: Chicken noodle soup with saltine crackers and a side salad as an appetizer.

DAY TWENTY-FOUR

BREAKFAST MENU: Bowl of raisin bran cereal with 2% milk and a banana or orange.

LUNCH MENU: Grilled chicken breast on a bed of lettuce with cherry tomato with cucumber, olives and light olive oil and vinegar dressing and a sprinkle of low fat cheese.

AFTERNOON SNACK MENU: A serving of carrots, celery and broccoli with light ranch dressing.

DINNER MENU: Baked fish, such as tilapia, catfish, perch, crappie, catfish, salt water trout or redfish with brown rice and steamed vegetables like carrots and broccoli.

DAY TWENTY-FIVE

BREAKFAST MENU: Whole wheat toast with jam, preserves or honey with a glass of milk.

LUNCH MENU: Beef tips with rice and gravy with a garden salad with light dressing and a glass of water.

AFTERNOON SNACK MENU: A banana and a glass of milk.

DINNER MENU: Beef fajitas with grilled onion and bell peppers on corn of flour tortillas with sour cream, light shredded cheese, refried beans and shredded lettuce and picante sauce with a glass of water.

DAY TWENTY-SIX

BREAKFAST MENU: Two hard-boiled eggs seasoned with salt and pepper with a piece of whole wheat toast and a glass of milk.

LUNCH MENU: Chili mac n' cheese with a side salad and a glass of milk.

AFTERNOON SNACK MENU: One serving of sliced cheese with crackers, mustard and a glass of water.

DINNER MENU: Baked potato with sour cream, chives, shredded cheddar cheese, chopped bacon (turkey or pork) salt and pepper with real butter with a glass of water.

DAY TWENTY-SEVEN

BREAKFAST MENU: Two soft-boiled egg with toast and 2 slices of bacon (pork or turkey) with glass of milk.

LUNCH MENU: Chicken salad sandwich or tuna salad sandwich with lettuce, tomatoes and celery and carrot sticks with ranch dressing or bag of potato chips and glass of water.

AFTERNOON SNACK MENU: An oatmeal raisin cookie with a glass of milk.

DINNER MENU: Baked fish with steamed vegetables and a side salad with a glass of water.

DAY TWENTY-EIGHT

BREAKFAST MENU: Two buttermilk pancakes with maple syrup and butter with one fried egg, a slice of cheddar cheese and one piece of turkey/pork bacon.

LUNCH MENU: Two pieces of fried chicken or 3 chicken tenders with fried potatoes or okra and one piece of bread/biscuit and glass of water.

AFTERNOON SNACK MENU: Bowl of raisin bran or cheerios cereal with low fat milk.

DINNER MENU: Oven roasted chicken with steamed vegetables and mashed potatoes with salt and pepper and a side salad.

DAY TWENTY-NINE

BREAKFAST MENU: Breakfast taco with sautéed vegetables, scrambled eggs, and picante sauce all wrapped in a flour tortilla served with a glass of milk.

LUNCH MENU: Sausage wrap with mustard, ketchup, or mayonnaise with a glass of water.

AFTERNOON SNACK MENU: An orange and serving of strawberries with a glass of water.

DINNER MENU: Homemade pizza with any toppings you want, such as anchovies, bell pepper, jalapeno pepper, mozzarella cheese, tomato sauce, green and black olives, pepperoni, ham, bacon, hamburger and served with a side salad with a glass of water.

DAY THIRTY

BREAKFAST MENU: Whole wheat toast with butter and honey with a glass of milk.

LUNCH MENU: An apple with a glass of water.

AFTERNOON SNACK MENU: A mango with either chili lime seasoning or plain with a glass of water.

DINNER MENU: Grilled chicken breast with steamed broccoli and mashed potatoes seasoned with salt and pepper washed down with a glass of milk.

DAY THIRTY-ONE

BREAKFAST MENU: Two fried eggs, any way you like and a piece of toast with butter and two slices of bacon: either turkey bacon or pork bacon.

LUNCH MENU: Club sandwich with bag of potato chips or sliced carrots and celery with light ranch dressing and a glass of water.

AFTERNOON SNACK MENU: Sliced melon like watermelon or cantaloupe, and a glass of water.

DINNER MENU: Baked buffalo wings with light blue cheese or ranch dipping sauce with a garden salad and a glass of water.

Guns Don't Pull the Trigger

As a ten-year old child and having possessed bb guns previous in life, I had two best friends that were country neighbors and they owned Benjamin Sheridan .22 caliber pellet rifles. I had a Daisy bb gun/.177 caliber pellet rifle, until I purchased a Brand New Benjamin-Sheridan .22 rifle from Academy Sports and Outdoors after saving money for almost 6 months....it was about $100.00. I earned the money from picking pecans, chores for my Mom and Dad and from cutting yards with a push-mower. I would hunt with the Benjamin Brothers for multiple species. They would always kill what they shot and what I shot would have feathers flying everywhere and no kills. I picked pecans, I picked dewberries, and I cut a lot of grass with a real old school push mower for months before I had over a hundred dollars cash. When I was checking out...I was short a little and my Mom chipped in and paid for the balance an d she got me the pellet bag and two cans of domed pellets. This was just enough money to buy a Benjamin of my own at Academy, but also some targets and some pellets. I preferred the dome pellets back then...now for small game I prefer the domed pellets....when something works...why deviate or make changes...stick to what works and you will never go wrong.

Actually, I just took my .300 WIN MAG scope, yes, the scope I took 6 boxes to zero at 200 yards, and I put that scope on my deceased

THE DEER IN THE WOODS AND THE FISH IN THE POND

fathers .22 Remington 550-1 and I sighted it in at 100 yards, bullet on bullet…and yes, back to my point, this is a great varmint exterminator, especially for squirrels that you want to put with dumplings and vegetables…and make squirrel and dumplings.

Well, back to the story…it was around Christmas time, which means duck migrating to the Southern States for wintering…just like the old timers come from upstate and fly to their homes in Florida….they are smart but it is called wintering nonetheless…and Floridians calling them SNOWBIRDS, and I learned that a lot of SNOWBIRDS come to Florida to winter and over half of them are recovering or struggling alcoholics. I went since I was in a treatment facility for the 10% of men that get sexually assaulted by another man or multiple men in the Military. I was struggling to hold it together when the other victors of victimology told their stories and how they would cry and we all would cry….it was kind of like exposure therapy verbally and visibly with real breathing human beings who were victimized and also strong in their resolve at coping and living with this for the rest of their lives. I kept my shit together towards the end of the program after three months of processing and having barely enough time to get ripped at the gym and a few trips to the Beaches in the surrounding area of Bay Pines, Florida. We had all been struggling for a while…unfortunately we kind of all lost touch or life…Cody, he killed himself just a few months after Bay Pines, and Greg is pissed at me for telling him that I was going to get a huge check for oil and gas royalties….I was testing him, he did not ask for money, and he never spoke of it…but I think that he was struggling emotionally or financially and got jealous in a good way. I was like a brother for Cody and Greg. Cody was really traumatized of being in an Airborne Unit and getting raped by a Senior Non-Commissioned Officer. Once when I told my story about being drugged just a week before coming home from a two-year long hardship tour as an Airborne Ranger and Air Assault Infantry Officer in a SOCOM or S.O.F. unit in Southeast Asia in the ONLY forward-deployed unit in the ENTIRE U.S. Military. I spoke of getting drugged and knowing of at least 5 of the guys who were Non-Commissioned Officers and Also a Fellow Officers.

Once they found out that being sexually assaulted as a TOUGH GUY and BILLY BAD-ASS and am in the same program as they were in. We were best of friends and would eat every meal, take every pass, grill together, watch movies together and lift weights together…fish together….and a little guitar playing and hitting the salvia divonorum when it was legal in Florida then outlawed…it was like weed, except it made everything look like cartoons. I could not help but laugh my ass off for over ten minutes straight.

I left the house after finishing my chores and headed to meet up after calling ####-830-##### to see if the brothers would want to hunt squirrels in the woods behind the airport. The feeling was that they were tired of sitting on the ground for squirrels that they would never eat or even much less clean. I convinced them that if we saw a rabbit or a snake that they had first shots at the target. I needed some meat to feed my family of five, yes, I was a teenager and had the burden of putting food on the table on a regular basis…so I needed two squirrels to feed 5 people, which basically means two pieces of meat per person if you butcher the squirrel into 10 pieces and freeze the other half so that you don't have to jack with the greasy and smelly cut up fat as hell full of steroid bagged discount chicken. This is why America is OBESE and out of shape. Squirrel, especially fresh and not frozen red fox squirrels and bled, skinned, saving the hides for making something cool after they were properly tanned, and the squirrel meat seasoned and sautéed in buttermilk or Italian dressing…for at least an hour then pan fried in butter in a heavy duty iron skillet until browned on all sides, then. Add water, potatoes, onions and carrots and celery then simmer for an hour on medium-low heat…just to keep it warm and it could be served with cornbread or flour tortillas or Kings Hawaiian Rolls…the best, but expensive…and totally worth it.

THE DEER IN THE WOODS AND THE FISH IN THE POND

We all met up 15 minutes later at our secret end of the world spot to link up and survive the mass destruction with pellet rifles, pellets, knives, and fishing gear for a lifetime and the knowledge learned in life to actually know what survivalists know. Carl had his dads pellet rifle from the early 60's and this was 1993, and the damn thing still had power and distance with every shot and Joe had a pellet rifle of the same Benjamin and Sheridan specs and was also a .22 caliber and then you have me…Totino Ramen, with a straight out of the box Benjamin Sheridan rifle and a cool pellet bag that I stored my pellets. Joe and I sighted it in at our secret spot and it took about 100 pumps for 10 good shots of the last three shots bullet on bullet…yes I said that… that's as lit as bullet on bullet…not only accurate, but also precise. Carl was sitting by his old faithful Oak tree with acorns all at the base and some chewed up acorn shells all scattered into a neat little pile of sorts, and he always saw or shot a squirrel….and I sat 30 feet to the south, or deeper into the squirrel woods and I was there for five minutes and I smoked a female red fox squirrel at about 35 yards. I bled it and bagged it and was excited that since I needed two for supper and I already had one. Then I heard a shot, it was Carl…he dropped one with his dad's old pellet rifle and it hit the ground with a thud. We bled it and Joe and I went to see if there were any turtles or snakes to be shot by the secret pond location….Called the Big Bass Tank.

Totino, or myself rather, had to get home to finish processing the freshly harvested meat and have it ready for supper…it was a Friday night so we went to bed later and it was already 5:30 p.m. so I needed enough time to have supper cooked and served at an appropriate hour to where we are not totally starving.

We shot at a few turtles cause everyone knows that turtles eat fish… well…that's what the urban legend is, but not all turtles eat fish…surprise…surprise…they eat vegetation. SO, I wonder how many harmless turtles we shot at our favorite fishing holes.

It took me about five minutes to skin, gut and process each squirrel and then the easy part…marination of the meat with my secret ingredients of Italian dressing or buttermilk then season with Zataran's or Slap Ya' Mama Cajun style seasonings which were added after the marinade/margination then have that iron skillet hot and ready for the squirrel meat, soaking in all that butter which will eventually be made into cream gravy for the biscuits that we are going to make for an accompaniment to this fine dinner.

Hunting is critical for a young boy to become a full grown man. It teaches discipline, respect, and safety when dealing with firearms. If every kid on Earth had this opportunity then I guarantee that there would virtually be no accidental shootings. I feel that schools should have licensed Psychiatrists evaluate kids from the earliest age of the domestic terrorist in America's shootings and make sure that the people unfit to own or have access to guns do not have this opportunity. I feel that this will at least curb the amount of shootings and ultimately the number of deaths and all that destruction will be non-existent or virtually eliminated. As an avid hunter, I own guns and I always have and always will. Even if I came up mentally insane or a risk, then I would gladly give up my guns in the namesake of keeping America, the Nation I almost died for while in the Army, safe and sound as good as can be. I feel that if every gun owner would have a Psychological evaluation before buying a firearm or every few years to get reassessed since mental illness can strike early or later in life. There needs to be reform of this sorts….just like pilots, military soldiers, they get regularly tested. If this would occur, I guarantee that gun violence would at least be reduced but not totally eliminated since there are ways to procure guns illegally or from private sellers and buyers. If we had more ways to track gun owners and they register all of their firearms no matter how old they are then we can really address the issue of gun control. As a Lifetime Member of the NRA and a prolific hunter, I would do this….even if it means that I have to relinquish my 50 plus firearms to the government or to a family member who is not diagnosed with a debilitating mental illness or I could sign then guns out when I am going hunting with another legal and law abiding registered HIP certified gun owner. I feel that the 2nd amendment needs some amending.....just like other laws and regulations....it's time for a change. This is my motto...."It's time for a change!" Please buy and read all of my books and I will use the profits for helping homeless Veterans and Battered Women and kids that have been neglected, abused and abandoned. Together we can change the United States and possibly the world. Thank you for reading my stories. Have a great day and remember, like smokey the Bear... ."Only you can prevent Gun Violence....Only You....and me too....so let's do this so we do not have over 300 documented shootings in our great nation....we are supposed to be leading the world in economics, diplomacy, democracy...yet we are leading the world in mass shootings and gun violence. Like I said..."It's time for a change!"

Mighty Mystical Magical Majestic Musical Mountain Maple Tree

In every country, every nation, world-wide on farms, in cities and in villages, there is magic just waiting to happen….as well as every young mind…magic is real…. you just have to believe and also have the most curious and inquisitive attitude and outlook with as much positivity as possible. For me, it is as simple as heading out to the woods with my faithful canine friend Ranger, a bottle of clear and crisp water and a bag of peppered beef jerky. I think better when I have a full stomach and am in good company like with Ranger…. plus, he loves jerky too…. he's more human than most canines. The water helps me to hydrate.... I suggest you do the same...no sodas or sweet drinks.... just pure and natural water.

Well, let's get back to the Mystical and Magical Mountain Maple Tree. It sits atop a very large hill in the country. It is located about one mile from the house....and it has many powers besides making good syrup for waffles and pancakes. You see, once a year nearby, a century oak tree produces acorns that the squirrels and other animals like deer eat.....there is a secret to having your magical tree come to full power....you have to pick a good acorn, pray on it and wish for whatever magical powers or whichever magical animal you would like to spend time with....the trick is to drink all your water, then put the acorn in the bottle, while filling the bottle with maple syrup from the Mighty Mystical Magical Majestic Musical Mountain Maple Tree. Once the acorn is covered in all that natural sweetness, you can now make your wish...it will come true if you really believe and have faith. This is the same way in life....if you have faith, in whatever you aspire to do... and work hard and really believe, then it will come true.

One day, Ranger has company.... seven kids that were all nieces and nephews to Uncle Beau, the owner of Ranger. They were visiting for a week or so since they were out of school for the summer. They all played volleyball, basketball, soccer, bad-mitten and also had time to get some fishing done. On the last day of the kids stay, Sophia wanted to visit the Mighty Mystical Magical Majestic Musical Mountain Maple Tree. Eliana, Olivia, Lily, Liam, Violet and Gavin all agreed that we should leave right before the sun set.... which is about 7:45 p.m. We packed two bags of deer jerky and 9 bottles of water.... we chose 9 bottles since it is Uncle Beau's favorite number and is more than enough water for our excursion/adventure. We set out and Sophia talked about magical unicorns, Eliana talked about flying horses with lots of speed and grace, Olivia talked about magical elves that would be able to fit into her pocket, Lily talked about swimming mermaids, Sophia talked

MIGHTY MYSTICAL MAGICAL MAJESTIC MUSICAL MOUNTAIN MAPLE TREE

about unicorns and rainbows with leprachauns with pots of gold that she was going to get after flying the unicorns to the end of the rainbow and using saddle bags to load and haul all the gold so she could feed the poor and have money to build them houses with nice furniture and nice clothing.while Liam and Gavin discussed that they wanted to turn mud into gold and silver so they could give the jewelry to their mom and grandmas and aunts for Mother's day. Violet wanted to have magical powers to heal her big sister Lily cured of her Charge syndrome. We walked for about 15 minutes, never taking a break while hiking all the way up the steep hill/mountain. Once we got to the Magical Mystical Maple tree, everyone was shocked to see so many squirrels eating acorns in the top of the tree which stood over 100 feet and was about 50 feet wide and had a trunk as large as a truck. There was bright green moss completely covering the huge and Mighty Mystical Magical Majestic Musical Mountain Maple Tree. Since we did not have a camera or phone to take pictures, unbeknownst to the group, Olivia brought along a sketch pad and some colored pencils....and she did a marvelous job re-creating the beauty of the Mighty Maple tree onto her sketch pad....she is quite the artist. Since we were a bit tired from walking so fast to get to the Mighty Mystical Maple Tree, we decided to take a quick break and eat some of our jerky and drink a little water. Since we are all family, we shared two bottles of water and passed them around since we were sitting Indian-style, cross-legged around the trees' trunk......since Uncle Beau was the oldest, he taught lessons on math and science while everyone snacked on jerky and drank their water. The lesson for today was centrifugal force and relativity of time.....it was boring, but Uncle Beau made it exciting anyway. As the kids were wrapping up their snack, Violet discussed how the tree was going to give her Medical Miracle Powers and she would be able to heal her sister. Since her wish was the most important, she went first. I instructed her to pick up a few acorns off of the ground and also pick a few fresh ones from the majestic tree. She picked them then put her acorns into an empty water bottle and then we carved a small hole into the trees trunk in order to fill the bottle with fresh maple syrup.

In about 2 minutes, the bottle was full and Violet was able to make her wish come to reality....she wished that she could have medical miracle powers and she got them almost immediately after making her wish.....instantaneously a Dr.'s medical bag and stethoscope appeared at the base of the tree....she already knew how to use the stethoscope since Uncle Beau gave her sister Eliana a stethoscope since she showed interest in medicine. Violet turned to her big sister, Lily and she was healed of her Charge Syndrome. It all happened so fast..... but Violet ended up graduating top of her class in Medicine and she is a World Renowned Cardiac surgeon in the entire Houston Medical Center.

Of The Hunt and of The Harvest

Chapter One---Preparation:

Selection of ammo...I suggest you shop for ammo and buy in bulk when it is on sale, and make sure you shop around and do your research, just like scouting, you need to shop around...otherwise it could cost you the same amount as a new hunting knife. Selection of eye and ear protection. Selection of where, how and who with you are going to sight the rifle in with. Then you sight it in and zero at bullseye at 100 yards flat. Next is cleaning your rifle and oiling it so you don't damage the rifle from sitting until the next deer season...which could be over 8 months-time.

Chapter Two---Practice

I would practice my grunt calls, my lifting of weight to mock lifting a dead deer onto the back of a truck, my rattling of antlers so that I might be able to grab the attention of that monster buck and finally concealment of scent and use of camouflage netting, tenting, and clothing so we could get as close as possible to make an easy shot and also building of brush blinds, tree stands, portable tree stand climber, box blinds and collapsible hunting tents used for Bow Hunting and also Black Powder Hunting. I practiced more and more as the season would near, but I never felt that I was that good of a shot until I was in college in R.O.T.C.. We shot M-16 rifles with .22 caliber adapter so that we could shoot indoors with no issues. I was the best shot that that Major in charge of us shooting and qualifying out of all the people he has taught or seen shoot. That really built my confidence. But those shooting skills from hunting in any stand type and preparing by research, seeing, acting, doing all the practice you can so that you make that "next hunt" A "SUCCESS HUNT!"

Chapter Three---Scouting...Kidding---Feeding...

This is probably the most important process besides sighting in your rifle or shotgun before going on a hunt. Scouting is easier now that we have trail cameras...you set a camera near a trail or near a bedding site to monitor times and weather conditions that the animals are moving the most....this will allow for better stand/blind set up and finding easy access travel points from your jeep/truck/car if it's a Subaru Outback....then you can enter your heaven nice and undetectable. I usually hunt close to bedding areas cause you get two times a day to hunt. You have a chance at success when they leave their bedding areas to go feed or breed and you get a second chance upon their return. Most big bucks are smart during hunting season and will only travel at night.... that's why they are the MUY GRANDE of them all.... and thus...the most challenging to kill with a bow, crossbow, long bow, recurve, shotgun, pistol, rifle, flintlock or percussion rifle. I prefer black powder and any bow, although your chances of success are markedly lower....it is such a great feeling when you harvest any animal in this "Fairer" game for your fare.

Chapter Four---Costs of Feed will Bankrupt You and can Make a Huge Difference.

If you live in a hunting area where baiting or feeding is not allowed, then I will say...you are a true hunter....In my neck of the woods we feed almost year round...things such as corn, oats, rye grass, protein feeds and if you have the money and time, food plots. Food plots are ideal for any cervid or bovine....and it is SOOO beautiful when you look see the green sea of grass, and it's more awesome when there is a light frost or a low fog.... then you know you will be successful....at least in regard to taking some really spectacular pictures. Feed and food plots cost money...so if you budget it out or have your hunting camp buddies/buddettes...and the children, you can all save a bit and split the costs.... this is the best way...but if you are on your own, just do what you can. Set your timers for three to four times a day for 3 seconds.... once pre-dawn, once dawn, once around 10 a.m. then one fifteen to twenty minutes before sundown...if you have feral hogs in the area, you will be able to see them on your game camera at the feeder. Since hogs are intelligent animals and are the closest anatomically to Humans, they are creatures of habit and if one comes, it is not long after that he brings his buddies. Feral Hog is delicious in sausage and for making bacon and hams. Plus, there is no open season or bag limit on hogs. You can get your feed that spoils and bait the hogs with this or save all your table scraps and put into a big container and bait the hogs with this stinky and foul mess, they just cannot resist. If you are blessed like me and my hunting buddies, there are Butchers that will process your deer. I recommend having it quartered before going there since most of them will charge for doing that. You can save even more money by de-boning all the meat. I personally save the ribs for BBQing...and the backstraps for making steaks that go along with biscuits and cream gravy and some collard greens as the veggies....and a soft boiled egg or over-easy pan fried egg and a piece of toast with homemade preserves or orange marmalade.

Chapter Five---Coffee, a Honey Bun Roll and a dip of snuff---THE HUNT!

Pre-hunt...you are all packed up, have double then triple-checked your gear and got up about two hours earlier than the alarm going off and were so excited that you forgot to grab anything to eat....so your hunting buddy is running behind....you got him using his truck because it is older and has better all-terrain tires....and also it saves you on gas money...kidding...but some people are actually like that. You get in the truck and spill your coffee reaching to turn the radio station....so you decide that you want a coffee from the gas station since Starbucks and Dunkin' Donuts doesn't open until 5:30. You get to the gas station and they don't have breakfast tacos so you get a coffee, honeybun and a roll of snuff. You get your buddy the same. You load up into the truck and head to deer camp.... good luck!

Chapter Six---The Wait

Waiting is a virtuous thing when it comes to hunting a is the difference between success and failure. I have learned that hunting natural areas where you cannot bait will make you humble for sure.... you generally pack a snack, a meal and water to last all day. You also dress appropriately and comfortably...and you wait...and guess what, wait...and wait some more.... until its early or late and then you actually know what hunting all is about. You might even fall asleep to only wake up to a deer or several deer in shooting range...I've done that a million times...well, not that many but I have done that a handful of times....hey if it works then I am going to snooze....and no...you snooze you lose only applies when necessary. I once fell asleep with one of my biggest hunting and fishing buddies, my cousin Hazim the Great. He has a blind that is Texas-sized... it is like a small efficiency bedroom that most New Yorkers would be jealous. I fell asleep since the night before we drank Jack, Crown, Dewar's, Hennessey or Jim Beam and Coke all night. Hazim does not drink but he does drink Cokes.... He even got me hooked on coke rather than beer or hard liquor. Well, I know I did this time.... I drank a whole bottle and later before going to bed at 0300, drank some of my friends jack and coke. So, at 0500, I am tired and groggy, luckily, I slept in my hunting clothes, except the jacket and boots.... I woke up and forced myself awake with about 9 cups of coffee. Hazim says, let's go and we both load up on the four wheeler. It takes about 20 minutes of driving, stashing the four wheeler and walking and setting up in his blind. I said wake me up when the deer show up. I laid on his carpeted deer stand floor and used my jacket as a pillow and he did wake me up...there was a hog....I grabbed my Remington Model 700 BDL and squeezed the trigger nice and slow and smoked this solid black sow at 250 yards....then fifteen minutes later on the Sendero I smoked a doe....we went back to camp with two kills and I sure was happy...Hazim volunteered to clean both the deer and hog, in that order. This year, I took my little brother with his entire family and he spot and stalked a deer at five hundred yards and got within 200 yards and smoked a good sized deer....we got almost all of it on video.....the deer was grazing in a ryegrass field....he was good because he learned how to do this in the Army and when he was playing Army as kids with my older brother and our neighbor friends. Good luck!

Chapter 7-Processing---Enjoying and Sharing the reward.... Being Neighborly

It is easy to process small game and also medium—deer and large game---elk, moose, bear, caribou and other larger animals like KUDU or Water Buffalo in Africa…..all you need is a knife with a sharp blade and a gut bucket and cooler for the meat….the gut bucket is for putting all the entrails/guts in there…this can be recycled for wolf or coyote bait…that kind of varmint hunting is exciting and also challenging. Back to the processing. You say a prayer for the animal before you kill it and after you cut its jugular veins on the throat…this allows the animals spirit/soul to make it to the next dimension…. it wards off the Devil and blessed your harvest. You load the animal up and then take it to a tree or some skinning area and gut, skin and quarter. For removing the head and cutting the legs off at the kneecaps, a Sawzall works well…otherwise you will hatchet it and/or use a machete…both effective but not anywhere cleaner and easier than with the Sawzall. You take the quartered deer and place in a cooler with ice until you get it processed. If you are in a cold weather environment, then you can hang the animal for a few days to age the meat…. unless there are bear or other predators that could snatch your harvest. That's about it…it's pretty simple and you will be so excited when you have quality meats to provide you, your family and countless others. Good luck.

Chapter Eight---Paying for Processing at the Butchers

Probably, you have a nice deer rifle or large game rifle…like a .300. win mag or 7mm mag…. or 30.06 or 25.06, you see my point, I could go on for a page…. bought your rifle for $600-$5,000.00 plus… and that was a hefty price…guess what…if you take your game to the Processor/Butcher, it will be expensive. I recommend doing the processing at home with your own gear…you can get this at Bass Pro Shops, Dicks, Midway USA, Academy Sports and Outdoors and other fine retailers. It's cost effective after the second and third season. I used to process my white-tailed deer years ago, so it made sense to get all the tools for processing…. I just don't have the time and I can afford to get them processed. When you open that pack of dry sausage and share it with friends at a sports game viewing, you will be filled with so much gratitude from them and they will be hooked on wild game as our ancestors were, when it was for subsistence and not so much for population management or for sport. Good Luck!

Chapter Nine---Shipping Dry Sausage and Dry Jerky to my Brother in Iraq for the 5th Time in his Short Career.

I sent about 30 packs of freeze-dried and smoked venison and beef sausage to him on one of his multiple deployments for combat against terrorism. It took three weeks to get there priority mail United States Postal Service. I had no idea that only 2 packs would not get there without getting molded in transit. He did give the sausage to the dogs in his Area of Operation. But if you are shipping meats, ask the butcher or Post Office Manager or Mail Man when he drops off you mail to your mail box…. really…yes…I have done this multiple times just this year…. but they will know the best method for shipping also FEDEX, UPS and DHL. They probably all will say freeze the sausage and pack it tightly in dry ice and then ship priority. GOOD LUCK! GOOD HUNTING! Enjoy the Brotherhood and Kinmanship and Sportsmanship.

Also, simple meals made by a Hunter.

Breakfast:

1. Pan Fried Backstrap and eggs with buttered toast.
2. Pan Fried strips of meat, bite sized and seasoned with Salt, Pepper, Worchester and cooked until tender, adding to a soft taco with scrambled eggs and picante sauce.
3. Pan fried backstrap with buttermilk pancakes with real maple syrup or at least Aunt Jamima brand syrup and a glass of fresh milk.

Lunch:

1. Deer Sausage wraps with mustard, ketchup or even mayonnaise wrapped in a flour tortilla or a piece of bread with BBQ sauce or plain.
2. Deer Steaks, marinated in Worchester sauce and pepper, marinated for two days then set on counter until room temperature then pan frying or grilling them with freshly grilled vegetables and rice or potatoes.
3. Deer stew with carrots, onions, red potatoes, garlic, salt and pepper with steamed rice or saltine crackers or better yet, cornbread muffins, all you can eat with melted butter! YUMMY!

Dinner:

1. Deer backstrap marinated in milk for 12 hours then coated in flour and fried in butter with a cream gravy and biscuits.
2. Deer Hamburger browned and served with all the fixing's for making tacos. Served with refried beans and homemade salsa and chips.
3. Deer sausage grilled on the grill or BBQ pit until the sausage is cooked and eaten with sauerkraut and hoagie rolls with potato salad and coleslaw or Caesar salad.

CPSIA information can be obtained
at www.ICGtesting.com
Printed in the USA
BVHW081603290421
606131BV00001B/78